A PIG IN PROVENCE

A PIG IN PROVENCE

Good food and simple pleasures in the south of France

·················

BY GEORGEANNE BRENNAN

CHRONICLE BOOKS

SAN FRANCISCO

Library of Congress Cataloging-in-Publication Data
Brennan, Georgeanne, 1943-
A pig in Provence : good food and simple pleasures in the south of France
/ by Georgeanne Brennan.
p. cm.
1. Cookery, French--Provençal style. 2. Brennan, Georgeanne, 1943-
3. Provence (France)--Social life and customs. I. Title.
TX719.2.P75B74 2007
641.5944--dc22
2006100180

ISBN-10: 0-8118-5213-X
ISBN-13: 978-0-8118-5213-5

Manufactured in the United States of America

Designed by Katie Heit

Distributed in Canada by Raincoast Books
9050 Shaughnessy Street
Vancouver, British Columbia V6P 6E5

10 9 8 7 6 5 4 3 2

Chronicle Books LLC
680 Second Street
San Francisco, California 94107

www.chroniclebooks.com

····· TO ETHEL AND OLIVER. ·····

··················

ACKNOWLEDGMENTS

This book, this life, could not exist without the people of Provence. I'm grateful to my friends and neighbors in Provence, and I hope they, like my family, will forgive any liberties I have taken with remembered conversations, meals, or events we've shared.

Donald, my first husband, began the odyssey in Provence with me and brought much into my life, and I will always be thankful for those extraordinary times we shared with our children when they were young.

I want to thank Bill LeBlond, a friend and my longtime editor at Chronicle Books, for having the vision of what this book could be and talking to Jay Schaefer about it over breakfast one Sunday morning. Jay decided to take the book on and has helped immeasurably to shape it, which was not an easy task, and never failed both to force me to do more and to encourage me that I could. Arielle Eckstut has proved to be the best agent ever for me, and I have much to thank her for. Judith Dunham, my copy editor, was invaluable. A special thanks, too, to Sharon Silva and Marianna Morgoraff for their help when this book was still only an idea. Thank you to Micaela Heekin, assistant editor at Chronicle Books, who helped move this book along at a steady pace.

My husband, Jim, has been my best friend, my biggest fan, and my in-house editor for more than twenty years, and has shared with me many of the experiences I recount in this book. He has read every word I've written at least three times, and somehow understands what I am trying to say, even when I don't say it right.

I wrote my first cookbook, *My Receipts*, when I was in second grade. My mother kept it, and when she died I found it in the old trunk where she stashed the mementos of her life. It has four wide-lined foolscap pages of crookedly penciled recipes, including Banana Snow (smashed bananas with cream), Rabbit-Pear Salad (a pear with almond ears and a maraschino cherry nose on a lettuce leaf), Orange Fluff (orange juice with whipped egg whites), and Strawberry Shortcake (cut-up strawberries over pound cake with whipped cream). The pages are stapled between two half-sheets of yellow construction paper.

I was a precocious seven-year-old in the kitchen, making abalone stew with my father and gingerbread houses with my mother. Later, I picked corn and strawberries with my boy-friends at the U-picks that used to flourish in the fields of Orange County, and made tarts from the apricots picked from the tree in our yard, getting the boys to cook with me. I cooked Thanksgiving dinner the year my father died, when I was sixteen, and I canned fruit with my grandmother. But it was the food of Provence, not California, that shaped my life.

In Provence I learned that food has a meaning that extends far deeper than simply cooking or eating it. I came to understand that the gathering, hunting, and growing of food is part of a life still marked by the seasons, a life that keeps people connected to the land and to each other.

Each season's food is anticipated: wild mushrooms in fall, wild asparagus in spring, melons and peaches in summer, and roots and truffles in winter. The people of Provence share an enthusiasm for the foods' origins. I realized that in Provence there is a collective understanding and appreciation not only of the food, but of the skills and knowledge necessary to grow sweet melons or tender young salad greens, to raise young lambs on hillsides of wild thyme, and to produce perfectly smooth, creamy goat cheeses, and that appreciation and knowledge comes to the table along with the food.

My neighbors in Provence showed me how to understand the land around me and what it could provide. They taught me how to gather snails and cook them, render fat, grow potatoes, and find wild mushrooms. They taught me how to grill sardines, make *aïoli* with a mortar and pestle, use leftover bread, make *pistou*, and choose a fresh fish. I came to understand that one lingers over a meal, that eating is an act of pleasure to be savored, just as is the finding of the food and its cooking.

In the life I began in Provence in my late twenties, making and selling goat cheese, keeping pigs, and cooking with my neighbors, I recognized that food was central to life, not for reasons of hedonism or sustenance, but because it was a link to everyone that had gone before me. It was a link to the land, a link to friends and family around a shared table, and a link to future generations to come. In a fragile, unstable world of change, food is a constant.

I never intended to become an award-winning cookbook author or to have a cooking school in Provence, or to teach Provençal cooking across the United States, or to have a vegetable seed import company. These things grew out of a passion for Provence, a passion for the people and for the life that food engenders there. And over all these years, Provence has never disappointed me. It, like the food, is a constant.

Obviously there have been huge changes since 1970, both in Provence and in my life, but the essence of our relationship remains the same. I arrive at the airport in Nice, flying in low over the Mediterranean toward the white city at the base of the Alps. I get my rental car and head west on the A8, past the high-rise apartment buildings, pounding buses, jammed lanes of cars, and palm trees until, just past Cannes, I feel a sense of calm descend on me. The rough red hills of the Maures on the west side of the A8 are undisturbed. The farmhouse on the east side is still there, its market garden intact around it. Forty-five minutes later I exit at Draguignan and start the drive into the interior. I think surely all will have changed since my last trip six months before. Provence can't be as wonderful in reality as it is in my imagination, I tell myself, preparing for disappointment. The land will be filled with billboards and housing developments, the vineyards pulled, the little villages diminished by suburban sprawl, the *cafés* closed, with no one eating long lunches. Some of this has occurred over the years, but it seems contained. I feel relieved when I see the familiar *cafés* full of people, the open markets packed with vendors and shoppers, the village shops still intact.

I stop and buy cheeses, ham, *baguettes*, and olives and continue driving deeper into the interior, through oak and pine forests, on smaller and smaller roads until I reach my house, set on the edge of a small valley.

The old stone house looms high and welcoming, and when I open the door it smells of fresh wax and wood smoke. My neighbors have left me a bowl of fruit and filled one of my vases with flowers. There's a note that dinner will be ready at 7:30 if I want to come. Year after year, Provence has welcomed me with food, camaraderie, and a sense of place and belonging.

Soon I'll be sitting out under the mulberry trees or by the fireplace with my friends, people I've known more than half my life, the people who taught me about life in Provence, sipping an *apéritif,* talking about the weather, the crops, the village politics, new recipes, and children. Then we'll move to the table, where we'll linger for several hours over a simple meal. If it's summer, maybe a first course of roasted peppers with anchovies, wild mushroom salad if fall, followed by a plump guinea fowl or an herbed pork roast, cheeses, and poached fruit or a tart. The rhythm of my days in Provence has begun again.

My hope is that through this book I can share with readers what has been an extraordinary life. The people of this deeply rural community welcomed me and my small family into their hearts, sharing with us their knowledge and the ways of the land where they and their ancestors have lived for generations. It was there I came to understand what role food can play in our lives, no matter where we are, and it is in this spirit that I have told the stories in this book, stories about meals, children, animals, food, places, and home. The stories are organized in chapters relating loosely to a central theme, such as goat cheese or pigs, or long summer meals, but all tell of a life of shared friendship and a passion for food.

CHAPTER 1

A PERSONAL HISTORY OF GOAT CHEESE

The first goats. Lassie dies. Advice from Mme. Rillier.
Reinette gives birth. Farmstead cheese for sale.

"How much are they?" Donald asked as we stood in the heart of a stone barn in the hinterlands of Provence, surrounded by horned animals whose eyes were focused, unblinking, on us. Ethel, our three-year-old daughter, held my hand. The animals pushed against me, nuzzling my thighs and nibbling at the edge of my jacket. In the faint light cast by the single lightbulb suspended from the ceiling, I could see the dark mass of goats stretching toward the recesses of the barn and feel their slow but steady pressure as they pushed closer and closer. My nostrils filled with their pungent odor and the fragrance of the fresh hay on the barn floor, with the faintly damp, earthy aroma of the floor itself, and with the scent of all the animals that had preceded them in the ancient barn. The heat of their bodies intensified the smell, and although it was a cold November day, the barn was warm and cozy. Its earthy aromas were homey and comforting.

"*Eh, ma foi.* It's hard to decide. How many do you want? They're all pregnant. They were with the buck in September and October. They'll kid in February and March." The shepherd, a woman, leaned heavily on her cane, making her look older. She was dressed in layers of black, including black cotton stockings, the kind you see in movies set in prewar France, her only color a dark blue parka and a gold cross at her throat. A black wool scarf tied under her chin covered her hair.

We wanted to have enough goats to make a living. Our calculations, based on the University of California and USDA pamphlets we'd brought with us when we moved to Provence a month before, were that a good goat would give a gallon of milk a day and a gallon would make nearly a pound of cheese. French friends had told us that we could make a living with the cheese produced from the milk of twenty to thirty goats.

"Why are you selling them?" I asked.

"Oh, I'm getting too old to keep so many. I have more than thirty." She looked around, then pointed at a large, sleek goat, russet and white. "I can sell you that one. Look at her. She's a beauty. Reinette, the little queen, I call her. She's a good milker, about four years old. Always has twins too."

She moved across the barn and grabbed the goat by one horn, put her cane under her arm, and pulled back the goat's lips. "Take a look. See how good her teeth are. She's still young."

Reinette was released with a slap on her flank and went over to another goat standing aloof from the others. This one had a shaggy, blackish brown coat and scarred black horns that swept back high over her head.

"This is Lassie. She's *la chef,* but getting old like me."

I expected the woman to cackle, but she didn't. Instead she

sighed and said, "She's getting challenged by some of the younger goats now, but she'll be good for a few more years."

Donald walked over to the goat and stroked her head. She stared at him with her yellow eyes and inky-black pupils. "What others are you selling?"

"Mmm. I could sell you Café au Lait." She pointed to a large, cream-colored goat with short hair and an arrogant look. "You might have trouble with her. You'll need to show her who's boss. She'd like to be *la chef*, take Lassie's place."

As if in response, Café au Lait crossed over to Lassie and gave her a hard butt in the side. Lassie whirled and butted her back, a solid blow to the head that echoed in the barn, bone on bone. Ethel pulled closer to me, holding my hand tightly, but kept her eyes on the battling goats.

"*Ça suffit! Arrête! Sâles bêtes!*" the woman shouted at the goats, menacing them with her cane. Lassie faced down the larger Café au Lait and the barn settled back into quiet.

"Why doesn't Café au Lait have horns?" I asked.

"Sometimes I cut them off when they're kids. I did hers. They looked like they were going to grow in crooked."

She continued her sales pitch. "Café au Lait is only three years old, and last year she had triplets. She's a good goat." She showed us four more animals that she was willing to sell and kept up her spirited commentary on their characters and fertility patterns.

Donald and the woman agreed on a price of 350 francs each, and he made arrangements to pick up the beginning of our goat herd in two days. We all shook hands and said goodbye, then wound our way back toward the square where we had parked our car. I made sure Ethel's knitted cap, a yellow-and-orange-striped one of her choosing, was tied snugly beneath her chin, then pulled up the hood on my jacket and put my gloves back on.

As we walked through the narrow *ruelles*, the tiny streets of the near-abandoned village, Donald quietly remarked on the ghostly feeling of the crumbling houses with their fallen roofs exposing rotted wooden beams and piles of fallen stones. Wild berry canes pushed through some of the ruins and fig trees had taken possession of others.

18

It was hard to imagine Esparron-de-Verdon as a thriving village, and impossible not to think of the woman and her goats living there as relics of the past, clinging to a way of life that was long gone.

Surely what we were doing was something different. After all, we had bought a farmhouse in the country, not in an abandoned village, and we were college graduates. Donald had a degree in animal husbandry from the University of California at Davis, and while we were going to make traditional French cheese, we would bring modern methods to our technique, or so we thought. I was a little scared, though. We didn't have a lot of money, and we needed to succeed.

First, we had to learn how to make cheese. Our USDA pamphlets, directed at large-scale commercial milk production and cheese making for the United States market, didn't discuss small-scale production of cheese from raw goat's milk. So far, no one, including the woman who had just sold us our first goats, had been able to tell me exactly what to do other than add rennet to milk.

"Mommy, can we have chickens and rabbits too?" Ethel asked as we passed a ramshackle chicken coop made of corrugated tin and chicken wire and utilizing the three remaining walls of one of the sturdier ruins. Her favorite toys were her rubber farm animals, and she was delighted by the idea of having real animals, in addition to our dog, Tune (short for Petunia), who we had brought from California.

"Shh," I said, "not so loud." The silence was strong and heavy, and I sensed it was best to leave it unruptured.

I bent down toward her. "Yes, of course we can. We'll feed the chickens every day and collect their eggs. And build a nice house for them."

I wasn't so sure about rabbits. Keeping rabbits meant having to kill them for meat. I knew that on a real farm, the kind we were going to have, you couldn't just have animals as pets. I wasn't sure I was ready for that part yet. I had no farm experience, having grown up in small Southern California beach town where surfing and sunbathing were the primary occupations. Chickens I could easily see—they had been part of my original vision when I imagined life in rural Provence, along with long, slow days of cooking, reading, writing, and sewing, with the occasional visit to Paris and trips to Italy and Spain, countries Donald and I had fallen in love with during our one-year honeymoon when we were students seven years before.

....

The first few weeks with our nascent goat herd were difficult, and we were on a steep learning curve. They wanted to roam and eat at their leisure, and we couldn't let them. The fields in the small valley below our house belonged to a farmer and were planted with winter wheat. He certainly wouldn't appreciate his crop being eaten to the quick by goats. On the far side of the valley, a vast pine and oak forest stretched to the north and west. If the goats ever reached the forest, we were sure we would never find them. That left only the hectare of land surrounding the house where the goats could feed, and that had to be under our supervision.

We didn't have an enclosure so we had to devise some means to keep them under control. We tried taking the goats out on leashes that Donald had made using thick nylon cord and heavy-duty, twist-top hooks fastened to their collars. They not only ate the grass, but pulled us behind them as they climbed the pear and mulberry trees next to the house, chewing on the bark, and fought to get at the oaks and juniper on the neighbor's hillside. I still have the scar on my knee from the rock Café au Lait dragged me over one morning.

Next Donald filled old tires with cement to serve as anchors for the leashes. The Americans' goat anchors quickly became the talk of the area as word spread from the postman whose brother owned the only bar in the village. No anchors could hold those goats, though. They would invariably head down to the field of appetizing green wheat, their weighted tires thudding behind them, with Donald and me following, trying to bring the goats back home.

We gave up on the tires and attached each goat to a metal stake we sunk deep into the ground. This was marginally more successful. Fortunately the cold weather and their advancing pregnancies made the goats increasingly content to snuggle in the warm barn and eat the alfalfa and barley we fed them.

We needed more goats, however, and someone told us that two shepherding brothers at La Motte, about forty minutes away, had some goats to sell. The Audibert brothers, legends in the area, could be seen during the winter months driving through the villages in their ancient black Citroën, the kind in old French gangster movies, berets pulled low on their heads, accompanied by their "housekeeper," a flashily dressed, dark-haired woman who lived with them.

They still practiced *la grande transhumance*, driving their sheep and goats on foot from the hot plateaus and valleys of southern Provence to the alpine pastures in the north for the summer, then returning to the valleys in late fall to overwinter the animals and let them lamb in the milder south. In the winter they installed themselves in La Motte, in a huge stone farmhouse with a *bergerie* large enough to hold the thousand head of sheep that made up their *troupeau*, or herd.

As we pulled up in front of the farmhouse, we saw the Citroën parked under the single, unpruned mulberry tree, with a sheepdog tied to it, and we knew we were in the right place. We went up the uneven stone steps to the partially open front door. The response to our knocking was a deep "*Entrez.*"

The room was lit only by the open door, a small window to the east, and the glowing embers of a fire on the hearth. As we stepped in, I was assailed by the odor of garlic and damp wool. One of the brothers sat at a bare wooden table, a bottle of wine, some bread, and dry sausage in front of him.

"Sit down," he said, waving his knife. "Some wine?" He got up and took three glasses off a wooden shelf above the sink. He was tall but not heavy, dark skinned and movie-star handsome, the kind of handsome where the dark shadow of a beard is omnipresent and the deep-set eyes are both vulnerable and arrogant. He was wearing a vintage black pin-striped vest and a wrinkled white shirt loosely tucked into black woolen pants, the style that men wore in the 1920s and 1930s, with buttons and flap. I could see a heavy, dark brown, wool shepherd's cape hanging on the rear wall where it faded into the soot.

I was transfixed by the presence of a power that came from the man's place in the *transhumance*, making the same treks over the same *drailles*, or trails, that the Roman shepherds had made two thousand years before. To me, the Audibert brothers and others like them were part of the living history of Europe.

After a glass of the rough red wine and a few pieces of sausage

21

plucked from the tip of the proffered knife, and after answering some casual questions about being Americans, we asked him about the goats.

"We're not going to do the *transhumance* anymore, so we don't need all our goats. Stay here all year. Settle down. Lots of people are doing that. Get tired of being up in those mountains. Good to be here. Got villages, music, *cafés*. Besides, people want lambs and sheep all year now. Used to be just spring." He sunk back in his chair, as if exhausted by such a long speech.

"Well, we're interested in buying some goats. We have seven, but need about a dozen or so more," Donald said.

"Come on, then. Let's go see them." He pushed up from the chair and grabbed the parka hanging behind it, leaving the shepherd's cape behind.

Donald, Ethel, and I followed him to the barn. It was built of stones, long, low, and sloping with a red tile roof, the kind you could still see then in the depths of inner Provence, where little had changed over the centuries and where people eked a subsistence living off the scrappy land. When we walked into the barn, the sheep, hundreds of them, fat with their winter coats, stayed bunched together, their bleating newborn lambs close to them, but the goats immediately came up to investigate us.

"Mommy, Daddy, look at all those lambs! Aren't they cute? Do you think we could get one? Do you? To keep the chickens we're going to get company."

"Shh. Not now. Maybe later. We have to get our goats first. Look at all these goats. Do you think they are as pretty as ours?" I had become quite attached to our goats once I had come to know their personalities.

Like our own goats, the Audibert goats were a mixture of colors and profiles. Some had horns, others not. Some had beards and wattles, others not. In our research on goats and cheese making, we had learned about the main breeds of good milkers: Saanen, Alpine, Nubian. But none of these goats we were seeing, or the ones we already had, looked like those, and when we asked about the specific breed, we just got a shrug. "*Ils sont des chèvres du pays.*" They're just goats from around here. I asked myself if these scruffy-looking animals would really produce enough milk for us to make cheese. It was clear that the first goats we purchased had lived a life of casual luxury compared to these goats.

Suddenly, M. Audibert walked away from the goats and went over to the huddled sheep and picked up something. "Here, this is for the little girl." He put a tiny black lamb into Ethel's arms.

"Feed it with a bottle. Warm milk. Its mother died."

"*Merci.*" Ethel beamed, saying thank-you in French as we had taught her to do, and cradled the lamb close to her, its gawky legs dangling beneath her arms as she stroked its silky coat.

"Look, Mommy, isn't it cute? He's soft too. Feel." She held him toward me to stroke. It was true. His coat was soft and smooth, but he was so tiny. I could feel his ribs and his little heart thumping beneath them. Ethel cuddled and talked to her lamb while we looked at the goats M. Audibert was willing to sell. We took all twelve of them, agreeing to his asking price of 250 francs each, 100 francs less than the first goats. I hoped we were getting a good deal. He said he and his brother would deliver them to us within a day or two. We shook hands and walked to our car, thanking him again for the lamb.

"Ethel, it's hard to raise orphan lambs. They get sick easily." Donald said as we were driving home.

"I can take care of him," she said, holding him tightly.

"It isn't just that. I know you'll take good care of him, and we'll help you. It's that their digestive systems are delicate, and

23

they get diarrhea. They get it so bad that they—that it's almost impossible to save them."

Donald had seen this happen time and again when he worked in the sheep barns at the University of California. I felt that I was the one being forewarned.

We discussed names and finally decided on Demetrius at my urging. I explained it was a Roman name and that the Romans had come to Provence a long, long time ago. We even had Roman ruins near our farmhouse, or so we had been told, and an ancient road from the Roman port of Fréjus to Arles ran through our valley, but we hadn't yet had time to explore it or the ruins.

As soon as we got home, Ethel took Demetrius to the barn and made him a special bed in an old wooden grape-picking box. She lined it with hay, then put a towel in it along with one of her stuffed animals.

"To keep him company," she told us.

We heated some milk and poured it into one of the tiny baby bottles Ethel had for her dolls. She cradled the lamb in her lap while she fed him. His soft mouth sucked on the rubber nipple until the bottle was empty.

"Look, Daddy! He took it all. Can we give him more?"

She was delighted with her success and enjoying the whole enterprise. Demetrius would be the first of many animals she would succor, from baby birds to pet rats and aging cats.

"No. We can't give him too much. Too much milk can bring on diarrhea. You can feed him again in the morning, OK?"

Demetrius never thrived. His legs remained too wobbly to stand on, and after three days he died. Ethel was devastated, and so was I. Donald felt bad for both of us, but I don't think he had ever thought the lamb would survive. The orphan lamb was our first loss in our new life as animal husbanders, and we buried him in a grave with an appropriate ceremony, Ethel presiding. She made a wooden cross for the grave from some sticks, tying them together with a red ribbon. Lassie died not long after, the victim of internal injuries sustained from Café au Lait's incessant butting. We buried her as well, but with less ceremony.

In retrospect, I've realized that we were living life much as it had been lived in the area since the turn of the century, when people depended upon the animals they raised, their gardens, and what they collected seasonally from the forests for their daily sustenance. It was astonishing to me, and remains so, that all the food I've had in Provence, from a wild dandelion salad to cabbage *gratin*, from *rôti de porc* to braised rabbit, always tastes so good, no matter how simple or how complex the dish.

The cooking and care given to food and its role in daily life stem from a not-yet-forgotten cultural understanding of the origins of the ingredients and an appreciation of what it takes to raise animals and crops and to hunt and to gather food, something I was just beginning to discover as Donald, Ethel, and I set about becoming goat farmers and cheese makers.

....

As the bellies of our goats swelled with their babies, we set about the now-urgent task of trying to figure out how to make cheese. When the Audibert brothers delivered the goats, I asked them how they made their cheese. They looked at me as if I were simpleminded.

"*On trait les chèvres, mon un peu de présure dans le lait. Le prochain jour c'est caillé, et on mon le caillé dans les moules. On les tourne le lendemain. Le troisième jour on les tourne encore et met du sel. Le quatrième jour ils sont faits.*"

In other words, milk the goats, add some rennet, let it curdle overnight, ladle the curds into molds. The next day, turn the cheeses, and the day after, turn them again and salt them. On the fourth day, they're ready. This seemed a little vague to me, especially compared with the technical material I had been reading from the United States, which presented cheese making as a very precise endeavor.

All that literature focused on the necessity of hygiene, pasteurization, and temperature control, and on the mechanization of the milking and cheese-making processes. Not even in *Mother Earth News*, the back-to-the-land counterculture magazine I always read from cover to cover, could I find any information about homestead goat's-milk cheese production.

There must be practical information available from local cheese makers, I thought. At that time, however, the young people who would form the basis of today's revived and flourishing goat cheese industry in inner Provence had not yet established themselves. I couldn't find anyone locally who made goat cheese to sell. As far as I could tell, most of the goat cheese came not from our region, but from other parts of France.

The charcoal-covered, truncated pyramids of *Valençay* cheese and the semihard rounds called *Crottins de Chavignol* were from the region of the Loire, and the *Cabécou* from Rocamadour in the southwest. Other goat cheeses came from Poitou, one of the largest goat-cheese-producing regions in France. None resembled the small, fresh, round cheeses that our friends had told us about, the simple-to-make farmhouse cheeses that we were going to attempt to earn our living with.

One day, as I was leaving the tiny *épicerie*, or grocery store, where I had gone to buy some rice, a woman spoke to me.

"I hear you have goats," she said.

She introduced herself as Mme. Lacroste. She was just a little older than I was, with shoulder-length, dark curly hair, a bright smile, and the work-roughened hands of a *paysanne*. I knew she was the wife of the man who owned one of the larger farms. They lived in a hamlet next to their vineyards.

"I remember when my parents had goats, and my mother made us fresh cheese. After the war she got rid of them. No one has goats anymore. I hear you are going to make cheese."

"Yes, but I'm having trouble finding out exactly how to make the cheese," I laughed.

"Do you want to meet my mother and ask her? I don't remember myself. I never made it, she did."

I accepted this very kind offer, and we arranged that I would come by her house that afternoon about four o'clock and go together to her mother's house.

Mme. Lacroste was sitting on her porch, knitting, when I arrived. She got up immediately to greet me, putting her knitting on the chair. "*Bonjour, Madame*," she said, and shook my hand.

"Shall we go?"

"Yes, yes, I'm ready." She was friendly, but seemed more abrupt than other people I had dealt with thus far, brusquely buttoning up her rust red sweater over a blue printed dress and picking up a willow basket lined with newspaper next to her chair.

"This way. My mother lives just down that road," she said, pointing, "at the edge of the hamlet. In the house I grew up in. And my grandmother too. I was an only child. Good thing I married a farmer. Those are our vineyards." She swept her arm in gesture that brought in all the vineyards in view, now shorn of their grapes and their leaves mottled with red and yellow. It was a large vineyard for the area, maybe four or five hectares.

27

The sky was a brilliant blue, as it often is in Provence during November and December, and a recent rain had washed everything, rendering the colors sharp and clear. It was strange to be walking down a dirt road with the wife of a Provençal farmer to learn about goat cheese. Not so long ago I was walking with other graduate students at UC San Diego, heading for lectures or classes across a new campus with modernist buildings of concrete and glass. Eucalyptus, bougainvillea, and long green lawns were the backdrop of conversation, not vineyards, olive trees, and forest.

As if she reading my thoughts, Mme. Lacroste said, "It must be very different here than in California. Is your family there? Your parents, I mean, and grandparents?"

My French was good enough for general conversation, but I lacked the vocabulary and nuances of the language to talk about personal experiences or abstract ideas. I haltingly explained that my father was dead, as were all my grandparents, three of whom I had never known, and that I didn't see my brother very often.

"My mother married again and she lives in Texas now," I concluded.

"How sad for you to have no family. Or almost none. I'm so happy to have my mother right here, so close, and my grandmother too, although she's blind now. Look, there she is."

Standing next to a sprawling two-story stone house was a woman in a bright blue scarf, holding her weathered face to the sun. Her black dress was indistinguishable from those worn by all the older women, remnants of a period when widow's weeds were required, I suppose, but her sweater was deep pink and her heavy gold necklace reflected the sunlight against her thinning skin.

"*Mémé!*" Mme. Lacroste called out, "I've brought a visitor to see *Maman*. An American. Remember the Americans? They came during the war."

Both hands were resting on the top of her cane. As we drew closer, I could see the gold bracelet on her wrist and a thick, worn gold wedding ring. Her eyes, covered with a bluish film, were set deep in her wrinkled face. Her thin cheeks rounded as she smiled.

"*Ah, ma petite! Comment vas-tu?*" She leaned her face slightly toward what she must have sensed was our direction, and my companion kissed her grandmother on both cheeks, and then introduced me.

"*C'est Madame l'Américaine.* She's keeping goats and is going to make goat's-milk cheese."

The old woman let go of her cane with one hand and stretched it out in my direction. I took it. Her handshake was firm, her hand warm and smooth.

"Yes, yes, I remember the Americans. One in particular." She laughed. "Very big and handsome, those American boys. Much better than the filthy Germans. The Germans took our house, you know. That's right. They were here almost six months, four of them. Ate our chickens, our food, everything. You can still see the bullet holes on the barn where they tried to shoot our pigeons."

The German soldiers had been right here, at this farm. What stories could be told, I thought. I wanted to ask her when they came and how they looked and what happened to them, and many more questions, but my language skills were not quite up to it. I also wasn't sure that questioning her on the subject at our first meeting, or ever, would be the correct thing to do, so I simply made some sympathetic sounds.

Many years later, when I was helping to serve lunch at a reunion of local *Résistance* fighters at the village *café*, I thought of Mme. Lacroste's grandmother, who died soon after our meeting, and wondered if the Germans who had occupied her farm had

29

been killed by one of the men reminiscing over the roast lamb and potato *gratin*.

Provence is like that. Whenever I am there, I bump into living history, all of it connected. I suppose I'm now part of that history too, the American who kept goats.

"Maman," Mme. Lacroste called as she headed toward the huge *potager*, the vegetable garden behind the house. There, her mother stood bent over a shovel, digging up what looked like onions. Rows of cabbages, greens, and beets stretched out around her in perfect symmetry. Every bit of the huge garden was filled with something growing. Like her mother, she was wearing a black dress, but her sweater was a somber, serviceable dark blue.

"I've come with the American, for you to tell her about cheese."

Mme. Lacroste turned to me and said, "My grandmother made cheese too, of course, but now, no matter what question you ask her, she only talks about certain things, like the Germans, her dead husband, her wedding trip to Nice."

"Bonjour, Madame Rillier," I said to my companion's mother. She gave me a no-nonsense handshake, and I understood where Mme. Lacroste had acquired her manner.

"So. You want to make cheese our way. No cheese in America?" She put her hands on her hips and looked me up and down.

"Yes, there's cheese, but not goat cheese. Not like the French homemade goat cheese." The term *artisanal* was not yet in my vocabulary. That would come twenty years later, with the beginning of the boom of artisanal foods in the United States.

"Well, I'm glad someone is going to make it again. No one does anymore." No wonder I couldn't find any cheese, I thought. No one is making it.

"I used to have seven or eight goats, milked them, and then made cheese," Mme. Rillier said. "I sold the extra cheeses. A few others around did the same. The others are dead now, and it got to be too much for me to do by myself. But I'll tell you how to do it. Come inside."

Mme. Rillier pushed aside the bowls of soggy bread and food scraps set outside for chickens, a dog, and cats, all of whom were hovering nearby, and we followed her through a swinging screen door into the kitchen. The dog, a brown and white spaniel, was on a chain, and the circumference of the ground within his reach was worn bare with his pacing. "We've got to keep him on a chain, otherwise he runs off. Loose dogs get shot. My husband goes hunting with him."

This was my first invitation into a family home kitchen since our arrival in Provence, and it wasn't at all what I expected.

No authentic-looking copper pans gleaming over a well-used fireplace, no exposed wood ceiling beams, no soapstone or red tile sink, no terra-cotta pots filled with olives, no bright Provençal printed fabric. In short, this was not like the kitchen in the farmhouse we had rented one summer outside Aix-en-Provence.

Over the next few years as I came to know various farmhouse and modest village kitchens, I would find most of them very much like this one. Many had been modernized during the 1950s or 1960s, with some indoor plumbing and electricity installed, and a small, tubular white enamel water heater hanging over a utilitarian white sink set in faux granite or tiled cement. The walls of these kitchens were painted with multiple layers of pale green or cream-colored enamel, and the floors were red tiles if old, or tiles of inexpensive granite composite if new. An oil- or wood-burning stove both for cooking and for heat was set where a fireplace had once reigned, with the stove's pipe cut into the chimney flue. Sometimes the mantel was still there, with the pipe stretching beneath it. Somewhere, there would be a propane-fueled, two-burner stove top or perhaps a modest new stove as well as the oil- or wood-burning one. Often, an overstuffed chair was in a corner and a small *canapé*, or couch, against a wall.

It was early winter, and Mme. Rillier's kitchen was warm. Something that smelled of onions and garlic was cooking in a hissing pressure cooker on the back of the stove. A stew maybe, or dried beans, I thought. Greens freshly cut from the garden lay on the sink, along with the bucket of onions she had just brought in. A collection of succulents sat in small pots on the windowsill. On the wall, above an overstuffed brown chair covered with a crocheted afghan in shades of orange, blue, and brown, hung a shotgun.

"Here," Mme. Rillier said, reaching into a cupboard. "This is a cheese mold." She held a cuplike ceramic object, glazed ocher on the inside, the terra-cotta of the outside unglazed. It was perforated with a regular pattern of small round holes. She reached deeper into the cupboard and brought out several more molds in various sizes.

"These are what I used. I think they might come in plastic now. Used to be someone in the village who made all the clay things we needed—*daubières, tians,* casseroles, bowls, and these cheese molds. He died during the war."

The war again. It was still close to these people's lives, I realized. She would have been about twenty-five when the war ended, and her daughter was born during the war. I wondered again about the Germans. What was it like to live in this isolated place, Germans billeted in your house, your men gone to war or with *la Résistance*?

"You make your cheese right after milking, while the milk is warm. Don't let it cool off. Pour the milk into a big bowl or bucket and add the rennet."

This was the key moment for me. I quickly abandoned my imaginings about the war.

"How much rennet?"

"Just a tiny drop for, say, five liters. Not much. If you add too much, the cheese will be like rubber, full of holes and bitter."

"And then what?" I asked, afraid that she had finished.

"Then you cover the milk up and by morning it will be curdled. Or, if morning milk, curdled by dinner. Scoop the curd into the molds and set them out to drain. That's what the holes are for. The next day, salt the cheeses, turn them over, and let them drain another day. That's it."

"That's it? What about aging? Isn't the cheese awfully soft?"

"Of course it's soft. It's a fresh cheese. Every day you keep it, it gets older. Cheese is a living thing, you know, like wine. It changes, just like us, as it gets older. If you want an aged cheese, you keep it longer."

This didn't exactly correspond to the USDA guidance about aging cheeses.

"But if your cheeses are good, you won't have any to age. People will buy them right away. It's hard to get fresh cheese anymore. And we all remember it, right, Marie-Pierre?" She turned to her daughter, who agreed.

"Well, that's it." Mme. Rillier put the cheese molds back into her cupboard.

I thanked her very much, and told Mme. Lacroste I could return on my own if she wanted to stay, which she did. I left mother and daughter in the kitchen.

The dog woke up to bark at me as I left, stretching and pulling on his chain. I stayed clear of his reach and made my way to the front of the house and back to the road slowly, trying to see as much of the *potager* as I could without appearing nosy. I kept my hands tucked deep in my pockets as I walked.

:::::::::::::::::

My second and last lesson took place in the sales room of a cheese-making supply depot in Lyon whose ad we had read in *La Chèvre*, a professional journal devoted to goats and goat products, primarily cheese.

34   There we bought a 50-liter milk can with a huge funnel, a three-part strainer, and paper filters for the strainer, plus 150 plastic cheese molds and 6 stainless-steel racks for draining the cheeses.

"You'll need these, too," the young man waiting on us said, pointing at stacks of heavy-duty white plastic basins and tubs.

"Is your cheese room free of dust and insects?" We didn't have a cheese room, and we were pretty sure we couldn't keep anything free of dust.

"No," I said, "not perfectly."

"In that case, I would recommend these basins with lids. They are very convenient." I looked at him and smiled.

"You see, as you are milking, you pour the milk from your bucket, through the strainer fitted on top of your milk can. Right?"

"Yes, of course. Right." Mme. Rillier hadn't explained this part.

"Then, I suggest you pour the warm milk into this plastic basin, add your drop or two of rennet, put the lid on, keep the basin in a warm place, and in twelve hours you have curds. The lid keeps out the dust and any insects."

He went on to explain that the curds should then be ladled directly from the basins into the molds, set on a sheet of corrugated plastic—he had that too if we wanted it—and the whey allowed to drain into a bucket or basin. He spoke next about the turning and salting of the cheeses, which didn't differ from what Mme. Rillier had told me.

We bought two basins with lids and a liter of rennet. Even though we would use only a fraction of a drop per liter of milk, we wanted to make sure we had enough for the milking season, which would be starting soon.

....

Our farmhouse wasn't completely ours. We had purchased it jointly with a friend, with the idea of sharing a calm, rural life with frequent sorties to the cities of Europe, while one or the other kept the house and the goat cheese business going. Very early on, however, it had become apparent to Donald and me that the communal life we had embarked upon with our friend, and now her new partner, was not for us and we began thinking about finding somewhere else to take our little family and the goats, a house with a barn and some land that we could buy. We talked during the long drive to and from Lyon and decided to tell our partners, Joanne and Guild, about our decision when we got back. We hoped that they would buy our share of the house, which they did. We bought their share of the goats.

In spite of the parting, we remained close friends, eventually sharing many summers together in Provence with our children. My friendship with Joanne spans four decades, two new husbands, three children, six stepchildren, and all the memories and experiences that form our personal histories.

....

Donald and I focused on herding our goats, just weeks away from giving birth, across the valley to our new house. It was a rental we had taken while hoping to buy something later.

It was in such a state of disrepair that it could have been called a ruin, but the roof was good and the rent low. It faced the southwest, and its ocher stones were bathed in light nearly all day, which I loved. The house had a well right beside it, and a fireplace inside, but no electricity. We installed new windows, a sink, a cooking counter to hold a two-burner propane cooktop, and a glass-paned door to let extra light into the single downstairs room that served as living room and kitchen.

Donald made us a bed with pieces of oak from an old, dismantled wine press and we set it up in the big bedroom upstairs. A smaller room next to it became Ethel's room. A door from the big bedroom led directly into the loft behind it, giving us easy, dry access to the hay we fed the goats. Downstairs we put in a similar door from the kitchen into the barn so we would have the same easy, dry access to the goats. I set up my small, screened cheese room in the space under the staircase, which was just large enough to hold the new draining and curing racks, plus a bucket to catch the whey.

Next to the spacious barn we built an enclosure for the goats, using sturdy branches of oak and pine from the forest behind us, so the goats could come and go freely from the barn, yet be contained. Donald fashioned a manger inside for their hay, and by the time the first kids arrived we were as ready as we could be.

When we were settled, we invited our new friends for dinner. Denys Fine, the local schoolteacher, and his wife, Georgette, both of whom were artists, had helped us with some of the work on the house. Mark and Nina Haag, an American couple we had met, were living in the village for the winter and had also helped us.

I grilled pork chops seasoned with wild rosemary in the fireplace. I had never cooked in a fireplace before, and although I relished the idea, I wasn't very skillful. Half of the chops were burned, partly because it was hard to see what I was doing by candlelight. The stuffed zucchini I cooked in my grandmother's cast-iron Dutch oven were overcooked, limp and shriveled, besides being out of season. Fortunately I had bought a nut tart from the *boulangerie* for dessert, and there was wine and good conversation. For months afterward we didn't have any more dinner guests, not because we didn't want to, but because we were too busy.

We had just enough time during the day to take care of our basic needs—food, warmth, clothing, and cleanliness, which meant hauling and boiling water and building a daily fire, among other things—and to tend the goats, milk them, and make cheese. However, not until Reinette had been in labor for more than ten hours did I began to realize how closely our lives were tied to the animals we kept in the barn just behind our kitchen.

It began with Ethel.

"Come quick! I think something is wrong with Reinette! Hurry!"

Reinette was lying on her side, moaning, her eyes rolling slightly back in her head. Donald had gone outside briefly and we called him back.

He knelt beside Reinette, gently pressing on her stomach and stroking her flanks.

"She's getting weaker and weaker. I'm afraid we'll lose her if we don't do something. I can't feel the kid moving. I'm going to reach up inside her. Maybe it's breeched and I can turn it."

I heated a kettle of water and Donald washed his hands and rubbed Vaseline on them. Ethel stayed right by us as Donald tried reaching inside the birth canal.

"I can feel it—I think I must be feeling its back. She'll never get it out that way. I'm going to try to turn it." She was bleating weakly now, but looked at Donald as if she knew he was trying to help her.

"I can't. My hand is too big. You try."

"Oh my God, I can't! I can't do that."

"Georgeanne, you have to try. She's going to die if we can't help her get that baby out. I think it's dead. We've got to get it out. Go wash your hands."

I tried, but my hand was too big too.

Donald turned to Ethel.

"Ethel, do you think you can put your hand inside Reinette like your mom and I did and help her get her baby out?"

"Yes," Ethel answered, her voice strong. She stood there, her arms straight down at her sides, looking determined. She wore the red-and-white-checked jumper I had made for her and the lace-up brown shoes she hated. Her hair was hanging down around her face.

"Wait," I said. "Let me tie your hair." She didn't like her hair back, but she let me put it in a ponytail and clip her bangs back with a bobby pin.

"You'll need to be able to see really well," I said.

Donald, slightly impatient, said, "Georgeanne, wash her hands. Then both of you come back."

A storm was coming and the sky was darkening, cutting down the already waning light. The first peal of thunder shuddered in the distance. The goats were restless, wanting to be fed and milked. I returned with a camping lantern and hung it on a hook we had put in one of the barn's beams.

"You ready?" Donald asked Ethel.

Ethel nodded. Donald put Vaseline on her hands and instructed her to reach inside and very gently see if she could feel something hard, like a leg or the head.

"I think I feel a leg," she said, her hand and forearm deep into the birth canal, her head pressing on Reinette's flank. "Wait. It's two legs. I think I can feel the hooves."

"All right, Ethel, now very gently pull them, ease them toward you. If we can get them close, then I think I can pull the kid out."

He kept rubbing Reinette's swollen stomach, soothing her. I did the same. She wasn't resisting us at all, just lying there.

"I got them!" Ethel cried, and fell backward, holding two severed forelegs.

"Oh, shit. The kid is dead and starting to break down," Donald said.

Ethel and I were both crying, she with her arms wrapped around my waist, her head buried in my lap, as we sat on the straw of the barn floor, crying from shock and for Reinette's loss. I took the bobby pin and rubber band from Ethel's hair, smoothing it, and held her close.

I hadn't expected this intimacy with life and death and wasn't prepared for it. It was different for Donald. He had spent five years at UC Davis, hoping to become a veterinarian. He had seen things like this before and knew it was part of the equation of raising animals. I knew it intellectually, but not emotionally.

We went to bed very late that night. Donald had managed to get the dead kid out, and Reinette had discharged the placenta. He gave her antibiotics and made sure she was comfortable while Ethel and I fed the other goats their alfalfa and barley and supplied them with water.

The next morning, the first thing on our minds was Reinette. We found her shakily standing, her udder hard with milk. Fortunately mastitis had not set in, and we were able to milk her to release the pressure. She continued to heal and eventually became one of the most productive milkers in our herd.

We left the kids with their mothers for two weeks, to give them a good start, and then we separated them, feeding the kids a mixture of powdered milk that we purchased by the twenty-kilo bag at a feed store an hour or so away.

It wasn't the goats' fault that my cheese was a failure. They were all good milkers and accepted us as their new masters, allowing us to put a bucket just behind their hind legs and then to squat down behind them and squeeze the milk from their udders. The udders were as distinctive as the animals themselves, and we came to know them by the shape and color of their mammary glands, and to learn the style and rhythm of milking that suited each. Some had long, dangling udders with teats that seemed part of the udder itself. These could be milked in one long, smooth squeeze, the jets of milk going directly down into the bucket. Others had plump, round udders, with small teats pointing out to the sides. These were more difficult to milk, and I often lost a stream or two as I tried to angle the teat downward toward the bucket.

Donald and I usually milked together, in the morning and again in the evening. We clipped the goats by their collars to the manger, where we gave each a half-bowl serving of cracked barley, a grain notable for increasing milk production, but not digestible if left whole. After each goat was milked, we poured the bucket of milk through the double-lined filter set on top of the milk can. As soon as all the goats were milked, we took the can of filtered milk into the house, poured it into one of the white plastic tubs we had purchased in Lyon, and added rennet.

The first batches of cheeses that I made were inedible, coarse and grainy, filled with air pockets, sour and bitter. Watching their progression from curds to cheeses, I had suspected they would be no good, but I kept hoping. It wasn't until the third day, when the cheese was supposed to be ready to eat and sell, that I admitted they were worthless. I took one to Mme. Rillier and asked what was wrong. She told me I had used too much rennet. I threw all the cheeses on the compost pile.

With the next milking I reduced the amount of rennet, using barely a drop for twenty or so liters of milk. I wrapped the plastic tubs of milk in heavy quilts to keep them warm during the curdling period, and I crossed my fingers. When I looked at them twenty-four hours later, the milk had not separated into curds and whey, but only thickened. When I tried to scoop it into the molds, it ran out the holes. It seemed I hadn't used enough rennet. I left it another twelve hours, hoping it would curdle with more time, but it didn't. It, too, went on the compost pile.

Finally, after more than a week of trying to get the amount of rennet correct and to keep the curdling milk warm in the basins, I had produced only inedible, unsalable cheeses. I tried to keep my mounting sense of desperation hidden from Donald and Ethel, and I kept trying. Finally, one day I unmolded a batch of cheese that felt different. Each round, dimpled with marks from the mold, felt firm and heavy in my hand as I turned it out for the final time. They were all sparkling white and looked appetizing, unlike my earlier efforts, which had produced gray to yellowish cheese with cratered surfaces, sometimes slippery with the beginning of pink mold.

I put one of the pristine cheeses on a plate and cut a V-shaped wedge. The interior was solid and smooth, creamy, and white, with not a hint of the air pockets I had come to dread. I tasted it. It was soft, slightly tangy, and very, very good. I called Donald and Ethel, who took tastes, and we danced around the room, holding hands. We had done it! We had made old-fashioned farmstead goat cheese! I got out our labels that had arrived a month before from Lyon, where we had ordered them. They were maroon foil, with a gold-embossed border and gold lettering with Donald's name, our address, and the fat content of the cheese, as required by law. At last, I had gotten the rennet and

41

the curdling temperatures right and had made cheese, really good cheese. Everyone had been right. It was a simple process—but mastering it had been difficult.

I put a label on every one of the two dozen cheeses, then carefully placed the disks in a shallow wooden crate lined with food-grade waxed paper. That afternoon I took them around to various people I knew to taste. Mme. Lacroste and her mother declared them perfect and each bought two. Georgette and Denys Fine swore they were as good as any they had ever tasted and bought three, one for Georgette's parents, who were visiting. Georgette took me up the road to meet Françoise Lamy, who bought two as well, and then to Marie and Marcel Palazolli's, just across the road from the Lamys'. Marie and Marcel were not there, but the door was open, and Georgette took me inside and told me leave two cheeses for them. They'd pay me later, not to worry.

The last ones I took, at Georgette's insistence, to a country *auberge* of some repute. The couple who ran it were formidable. She was said to be a harridan, he a sweet and charming alcoholic.

It was four o'clock in the afternoon, after the lunch hour and, I thought, a good time to call. I walked up the rear steps that led to the restaurant kitchen, as Georgette had instructed me to do, and before I could knock, the door swung open.

"Yes? What do you want?" asked a tall woman with a curly topknot of orange hair and heavily mascaraed eyelashes, thrusting her face toward me.

"Georgette sent me. I'm the American with the goat's-milk cheese. She thought you'd like to try some."

"What about Georgette and cheese?" a male voice called from the background. A tall, thin man dressed in chef's whites came to the door. He looked at the box of cheeses I held and asked me to come in.

The woman shrugged her shoulders and stepped back. "*Entrez.*"

I entered and there before me was a Provençal kitchen. It had heavy wooden ceiling beams, with hanging copper pots and pans of varying sizes. A fireplace was set in one wall, its embers still glowing. A long, black spit was operated by a series of weights and counterweights. Terra-cotta *gratin* dishes were stacked next to big soup pots, and shelves held a collection of Provençal plates and platters in green and ocher. The remains of a meal, theirs I assumed, was spread out on one end of a long, heavily scarred wooden table that ran nearly the length of the room. The other end held a brace of unplucked pheasants.

"Here. Put the cheeses here," the man said, offering me his hand. "I'm M. Duvivier; my wife, Mme. Duvivier." We all shook hands.

"Sit down, sit down," he gestured, putting a chair between the lunch remains and the pheasants. "Would you like coffee? We are just having some." I accepted, and we had some small talk before he said, "Now, let's sample the cheese."

He took a knife, and as I had done, cut a wedge, first for his wife, then for himself. They were quiet when they finished. My heart sank. If these people, experts of the *terroir, gastronomes*, didn't like my cheeses, I didn't know what I would do. I hated Georgette for sending me there. I could feel my chest tightening, a sure sign that tears were not far behind, and I got up to leave.

"Sublime. Truly sublime!" M. Duvivier cried. "How is it possible that an American could make such a French cheese? I'll take them all to start with, then we'll see. I'll age a few myself, have others fresh, yes, yes, local cheese. Wonderful!" He grabbed both my hands in his.

43

Mme. Duvivier smiled. "Yes, it's very good, my dear. Very good indeed. And if my husband likes it, it is a great compliment. He is very particular, you know. That is why people come here, from Paris even, to eat his food."

I left the cheeses with them, accepted the thirty-two francs fifty they gave me, and headed home, excited about telling Donald and Ethel the good news about our cheeses.

Soon I was selling our cheeses to the *auberge* and the local *épicerie*, and at the Saturday market in Barjols and on Wednesdays in the square of a small village where I was the only vendor and people came out of their houses just for my cheese.

On market day I got up at five to milk the goats and do my cheese work before packing my cheeses onto the racks stacked in the back of the *deux chevaux camionette*, our little bluish gray van, circa 1958. Once at the market I set up the table at my designated location on the square and displayed my cheeses, putting a label on each before covering them with white plastic mesh to protect them from dirt and insects.

As people bought my cheeses, I wrapped them in parchment paper, took the money, and put it in a small metal box. I quickly had a following of customers, and as word got around that we had fresh goat's-milk cheese, people would even find their way to our house to buy them, sometimes a dozen cheeses at a time, making the bumpy journey over the dirt road and across the trickle of stream to get to us.

....

We stayed in the house by the forest with the goats, and soon a pig, through the spring and summer, and into early fall. But, especially when I became pregnant, it was clear that we couldn't live there through the winter. Rain sometimes made the road impassable, the fireplace didn't provide enough heat, and with the shortening days, nightfall came quickly.

Our friends Denys and Georgette Fine offered to rent us a place on their property, a house of three small rooms, a kitchen and two bedrooms, that they called *la cellule,* the cell. Their property had once been a tile factory, and they had created the little house from the ruins of the vats where the clay had been stored, eventually living there with their two sons while restoring the main house next door. We decided to accept. We could continue to keep the goats and the pig where they were, going back and forth across the valley to tend them.

I loved my new kitchen. It was cozy, with a woodstove, a glossy red-tiled counter fitted with the usual two-burner cooktop, a round limestone sink with running water, and a built-in table with artistically sculpted white plaster benches on three sides. A large cupboard, partially screened in the rear to let in cold air, served first as our refrigerator and later as a cheese-curing cupboard. There was even a large, outdoor summer kitchen with an ivy-covered roof. A red-tiled walkway ran the length of the house and gave onto a broad yard bordered with bay laurel trees, rosemary, and the remnants of a stone wall.

As winter began to descend, and the baby's due date approached, I started making thick vegetable soups and stews, simmering them on the back of the woodstove for hours at a time. Ethel, standing on top of a footstool, made her first pancakes using the cooktop. My kitchen was always fragrant with the wild thyme and rosemary I had gathered and hung from the rafters. At night, Donald read stories aloud to us as I cooked dinner and Ethel drew or played with her toy animals, our dog, Tune, curled at her feet. It was, at last, the beginning of home.

45

Salade au fromage du chèvre avec croûtons frites

GOAT CHEESE SALAD WITH FRIED BREAD

When I'm in Provence, I make this salad all the time because I love the goat cheese there so much. I make it in California, too, but a medium-dry goat cheese is hard for me to find. Be sure to use extra-virgin olive oil for frying the bread. It makes a big difference.

Begin by frying a *baguette* slice or two in a little olive oil until golden, turning the bread once, and adding a clove or two of minced garlic. In a salad bowl, pour enough olive oil to cover the bottom in a thin layer. Add enough red wine vinegar to cover about a third of the olive oil, sprinkle in two or three pinches of coarse sea salt, and just slightly less freshly ground black pepper. Mix with a fork.

www.frenchgoatscheese.com

Next, add some torn leaves of escarole, *frisée*, lettuce, arugula, or whatever other greens bought at the market that morning or collected from the garden. When I'm making the salad for myself, I use about two big handfuls, three if it's going to be my main dish. Finally, put half of a *demi-sec*, or medium-dry, goat cheese—one that is about ten days old—under the broiler, cut-side down. Take the cheese out when it begins to melt slightly around the edges. After tossing the salad, heap it onto a plate and sprinkle it with the crisp garlic. Arrange the fried *baguette* slices on the salad and, if it's summer or early fall, add a thick slice of tomato, then slip the warm cheese on top.

MAKES 1 SERVING

CHAPTER 2

A PIG IN PROVENCE

Encounters with M. Gos. Lucretia's piglets. A harvest lunch.
La mise à mort. *Provisions.*

When we bought our pig from M. Gos, we didn't know that we were about to become participants in one of the region's longtime subsistence rituals. Donald had worked at the pig barns, as well as the sheep barns, at UC Davis and had always wanted to keep pigs. So buying a sow and raising feeder pigs seemed like a good idea, and would fit in with our cheese making since we could mix the high-protein whey with the bran the pigs would eat.

"I don't know," said M. Gos, pulling his blue cap down a little lower on his head as we walked toward a low-slung stone building. "Sows are delicate. Sensitive. You have to be gentle with them." He lifted the metal latch of the barn's heavy wooden door and pulled it open. Had there not been stout metal rails around the pens, we would have been stampeded. A half-dozen or more huge pigs came pounding toward us at full speed. They snorted and shoved, and blinked their pinkish eyes rimmed in stiff white eyelashes, struggling to get at their master, who in turn scratched each one behind the ears.

"*Ma chérie, oui, oui, je suis ici. Ah oui, tu es belle, toi aussi.*" He turned to us, smiling. "See how beautiful they are. Very affectionate." Donald also loved pigs, finding them, just as M. Gos did, sensitive and interesting. He knowingly scratched their ears. Unfamiliar with pigs, I stood by quietly, a little frightened by the big, powerful beasts, while Ethel intently examined the snuffling, pink-snouted animals from the security of her position behind my back.

M. Gos next took us around to the far side of the barn, where we were greeted with squeals and squeaks as a jumble of piglets spilled over each other at the trough just inside their pen, scrambling to get to us. M. Gos reached over and picked one up by the scruff of its neck and handed it kicking and squealing to Donald, who readily took it in hand. He offered it to me, and I tried to take it in my arms as I would a kitten or puppy, but it twisted and squirmed.

"No, no," they both cried at once, grabbing the scruff of its neck.

"You have to hold it like this," said Donald, illustrating a maneuver that seemed a bit brutal to me but worked. I could barely hang on. The pig was a small, solid chunklet of energy, with every fiber of its little body bursting beneath its bristled skin. I held it as tightly as I could, wrapping my arms around it as it twisted, squirmed, and squealed. I was terrified it would spring out of my grasp, even though I held tightly to the scruff.

"Here, please take it," I said to Donald with a weak but enthusiastic smile for M. Gos, who smiled and nodded, taking the piglet from Donald and returning it to its siblings.

We stood together, elbows on the railing. M. Gos pulled out a pouch of Gauloise tobacco and a packet of cigarette papers.

He offered them to us. I accepted and we both rolled a cigarette, licking it sealed. He pulled a hard candy out of his pocket and offered it to Ethel.

"Pigs really are intelligent," he said. "I've had at least one pig all of my life. Except when I went to Paris. I was young then. It's a beautiful city. But I came home." He lit our cigarettes. "My son likes the grapes and the fruit trees, but he's not very interested in pigs. His wife isn't from here. Where are you from?" He turned to look at us.

"We're from California," I answered. Donald explained that he had grown up in San Francisco, but that we'd been living in Southern California, where we'd been going to a university.

"What did you study?"

"Agriculture first, then philosophy. Georgeanne studied history."

"Hmmmm. Why did you come here?" M. Gos asked.

It wasn't hard to have simple conversations about the weather, animals, or agriculture in French. But trying to explain why a philosophy Ph.D. candidate and a history Ph.D. student at the University of California at San Diego and their small daughter had thrown over their lives to buy a farmhouse and a little land in Provence so that they could make goat cheese was a different matter.

"I went to the university in Aix-en-Provence. We got married in Aix and always liked France. Since the war in Vietnam is making life so hard in the United States, well, we thought we would try to make a life here," I said, holding Ethel's hand tightly. That was as close to an explanation as I could give.

"Hmmmm." M. Gos put out his cigarette, then slipped the butt in his pocket. "You have a nice spot for a pig over at your place, there with the goats. I'm retired now, and getting old.

It's too much to keep all these sows. I've got a lot of customers, though. They depend on me for a pig to raise every year to *faire les provisions*—to make the hams, *pâtés*, everything. No one else around anymore sells little pigs. Only me. I don't want to disappoint people."

He turned back toward his house. "You're thinking about raising a few pigs, then?" Donald had explained earlier about his background, and I could tell M. Gos knew that Donald understood pigs, even without talking about it.

"*Bien.* We'll see. Come and have a drink." We followed him back to his house in the hamlet, more or less up and over from the barn. His wife opened the door and smiled, motioning to us to sit down. She was short and stocky, like so many local women of her age and generation, with soft gray hair pulled into a tidy bun at the base of her neck.

The pale green Formica table in the kitchen was set with a clear glass wine bottle full of water; a bottle of pastis; a bottle each of grenadine, *menthe*, and *orgeat* syrup; and five small glasses. The kitchen was filled with the scent of tomatoes and sausage, which I assumed was coming from the orange enamel casserole simmering on the stove. It would be noon shortly, and I knew that as soon as we left, the couple would sit down to what was probably an unctuous stew, preceded by some slices of homemade *jambon cru*, *pâté*, and fresh bread. We, on the other hand, would go home to noodles topped with sautéed onions, garlic, and carrots, all well seasoned with wild rosemary and olive oil. Our budget in those days allowed for little meat.

"Please, sit down," M. Gos said, and we all took a seat. Ethel was served first. At three years old and just over six months in France, she could speak a few polite words of French and when asked what she wanted to drink replied "Grenadine, *s'il vous plaît*."

"*Préférez-vous un tomat, perroquet, ou mauresque?*" asked M. Gos, turning to us now. Seeing the rather blank look on our faces, he laughed. "When you mix *pastis* with grenadine, it's a *tomate. Pastis* and *menthe* make a *perroquet,* and *orgeat* and *pastis* are a *mauresque.*" I didn't know what *orgeat* was.

"It's almond-flavored syrup. The story goes that the Moors brought the almonds to Provence so that's why we call it a *mauresque.*" His wife beamed at him, touching his large hand as he poured our choices. He poured for her, without asking, a little *orgeat* and water. "*Salut,*" he said, and we all drank. He took off his cap, revealing wisps of gray hair on a pink, balding head. "I'll come over tomorrow and look at your *cochonnerie* to see if it will work for one of my young sows."

We thanked M. and Mme. Gos for our drinks and stood up to go. It was almost noon, and politeness requires that you excuse yourself when it is mealtime. "Wait a minute," M. Gos said. He opened a door off the kitchen and came back with a small glass canning jar of *pâté.* "Try this." We said thank you again, shook hands, and went home, driving down the packed dirt road that led out of the hamlet onto the main road toward home.

Once there, we released the wire clasp holding the lid on the jar and looked inside at the ball of coarse *pâté,* all but the uppermost round covered with creamy white lard. Donald sliced the bread we had picked up on the way back and set it on the table along with the *pâté.* I put out some *cornichons,* and we sat down. I spread a slice with a little lard, then topped it with *pâté,* the way I had seen others do, and gave the slice to Ethel, who promptly ate it and asked for more. We didn't finish the whole jar, but we could have.

After several more visits, more *pastis* sharing, and more conversation, M. Gos decided to sell us one of his young sows. That meant that we would have a brood sow, one that we would keep

53

for years. She would be a pet, so we would name her. Brood sows were kept for the purpose of providing babies, and a good sow would have two or three litters a year, each averaging twelve babies. These were sold at about six weeks old to farmers as feeder pigs—that is, pigs to be fed for a year and then slaughtered for meat. Brood sows didn't go to slaughter until they were too old to breed, and that could be as many as five or six years.

"You can breed her again in a few months. Bring her to my boar. She'll have babies four months later. That's good, because they'll be ready to sell in five to six weeks. I'll tell my customers to go see you. By the way, if you want some firewood, just come by. I've got extra this year."

M. Gos became our friend, coming by to see us and the pig we named Lucretia. He was especially fond of Ethel and always had a bit of candy or chewing gum in his pocket for her and often something for us as well. He was delighted to see that I was going to have another baby and always asked how I was feeling. Once, shortly after we had acquired Lucretia, he brought us several links of *boudin noir*, fresh blood sausage, that he had made and some fresh pig's feet. I had learned to love *boudin*, after sampling it under duress at a dinner one night at the Fines' house, our landlords and now our good friends. I was delighted to have the sausages again. That night I fried them slowly in butter, letting the edges darken and crisp. I served them with cooked apples and mashed potatoes, as I had been taught by Georgette.

I didn't know what to do with the pig's feet, so I went next door and asked Georgette. Nine years older than I was and a whirlwind of energy, she seemed to be perfectly in tune with the rhythms of rural life and to know everything about it. "Split each foot in half and poach them, tied up in cloth, for about five hours. Then let them cool, take off the cloth, and put olive oil all over them. Make a mix of bread crumbs, salt, pepper, and herbs and pack this all over the feet. Then fry them. Ahhh." She closed her eyes and smacked her lips.

Since I could not imagine myself slicing up the smooth, white, cloven, cartilaginous feet and then eating them, I gave them to her, explaining I didn't think I would have time to cook them. (I still had intense memories of *Erbsensuppe mit Spitzbein*, which I had ordered once in Berlin. The bean soup was rich and creamy, but the whole foot sticking out of it had a smattering of hairs, and I didn't know how—or if—to eat it.) I should have known when the normally generous Georgette did not bring back a sample of the fried pig's feet that I had missed out on something tasty.

Later I came to understand that we had been the recipients of the traditional *don*, or gift of pieces of meat given to family and neighbors once a pig has been slaughtered. The annual winter slaughter of pigs was staggered over a month to six weeks, allowing small rural communities to have fresh meat when such a commodity was scarce. It was also a time to extend and renew friendships. In the strictest sense, the tradition called for giving certain pieces or preparations to neighbors and family who were not invited to the festive midday meal that celebrated the slaughter day. These gifts were distributed according to the village social hierarchy, of which every one was acutely aware. During our first years in Provence, the tradition was still carried on, even though the necessity was long past, and I think we were among the last to experience it.

Lucretia's first litter was fourteen piglets, each the size of a large hand. When I went out to her pen and found it full of baby pigs, I was terrified. I watched her roll over and crush two of them as she struggled to get comfortable, and could see more caught

55

beneath her. There was nothing I could do, and I couldn't reach Donald because he was off delivering chickens to Toulon, part of a job he had taken to supplement our income. I drove as fast as I could to M. Gos, Ethel with me, for help. He came immediately, bouncing down the dirt road to our barn right behind us in his little Renault.

"Now, now my beauty, yes, my love, you'll be fine. What a lovely mother you are. Such lovely little babies you have. Yes, you've done a good job." He stroked Lucretia as he gently repositioned her so he could remove the dead babies from beneath her and push the others to safety in the corner. He stood up.

"She'll become calm in a little bit. There girl, now, now. That's my girl. Yes, *chérie*, good job, good job. Lovely little babies. Yes, that's right," he cooed as he guided her down on her side, teats exposed. The little pigs scurried over, and after much scrambling and confusion, each attached itself to a teat and settled into quiet sucking. M. Gos and I added fresh straw to Lucretia's bed.

"Don't feed her quite yet. If she sees food in the trough she'll want to get up and might step on one of the babies. Wait a few hours." We talked a bit more, and he gave Ethel a Malabar bubblegum, her favorite because it had a little comic strip inside. When Donald came home that night, he went immediately to Lucretia to feed her and to see the babies. One more was dead. Of the litter of fourteen, eight survived, one more dying a few days later when Lucretia stepped on it.

Lucretia rapidly became a pet, and she responded to us just as I had seen M. Gos's pigs respond to him. I, too, began talking to her, calling her sweet names, and spoiled her with treats like fallen pears and almonds that I gathered from abandoned trees. She loved the whey we fed her, and the bran, and soon her little piglets were lapping it up as well. They quickly grew into handsome creatures, and Donald performed the necessary castration on the males.

"Got to do it," M. Gos told us on one of his friendly inspection tours. "Otherwise, no one wants them. Their meat gets too strong." Donald had performed the procedure frequently at Davis, so he was perfectly at ease when the time came to castrate our five males. I, on the other hand, was not. I did manage to fulfill my role as assistant with dignity as well as trepidation, and our perfect little pigs were soon ready for sale as feeder pigs.

M. Gos sent several of his regular buyers to us. "Old Gos says these are good pigs," said our first customer, an elderly farmer dressed in layers of brown clothes. As he leaned over the rails to look at the pen of little pigs, he explained his confidence in us. "Gos told me you bought the sow from him, bred her with his boar, and that you feed them whey from that goat cheese you make. That true? Got any of that cheese?" We sold him some cheese and two piglets. The rest of the piglets were soon sold as well, and shortly thereafter Lucretia visited the boar again.

As winter approached we began to hear more and more about the coming *jour du cochon*, the day when the family pig is killed, *pâtés* are made, hams and bacon are salted, and a big feast, attended by family and friends who helped with the work, is held in honor of the occasion. In Provence, the *jour de cochon* is associated with Saint Antoine, Saint Vincent, and Notre-Dame, because their feast days fall from the middle of January to the beginning of February, the coldest time of the year, when the pig must be killed and the meat given time to cure before the weather warms. If not, the meat will spoil.

Marie and Marcel Palazolli, tenant farmers of Italian descent who lived just up the road from us, were well known for the quality of their pork provisions, which they made from the succession of pigs they fattened each year.

Everyone liked to harvest grapes for Marie and Marcel because of the lunches Marie, one of the best cooks I have ever known, served to the crew. Marie was short, with golden olive skin, dark hair kept short, and a rumbling laugh that began as a deep chuckle. She always wore an assortment of sweaters, vests, and caps or scarves, the type depending on the weather, and her hands were as creased and worn from hard work as Marcel's. She looks just the same today, only her hair has a reddish tint, like mine. Marcel's hair was already gray when I first met him—it's pure white now—and his delicately boned face has rosy red cheeks and bright blue eyes. Back then he usually dressed in the standard blue worker pants and jacket with a heavy sweater underneath, and a wool cap as needed. Today, he's more likely to be seen wearing Nike sweats and a logo baseball cap.

The harvest lunches began promptly at noon. Marie picked grapes until eleven, then went home to finish the meal so that everything was ready when the workers, about ten in all, Donald and me included, tromped up the narrow, twisting staircase that led to Marie and Marcel's apartment in the huge, old stone farmhouse. Once owned by a single family, the house had since been divided between three owners, one of them the proprietor of the land Marcel farmed. Marcel and Marie got the apartment as part of their land tenancy contract.

After the workers sat down around the large Formica kitchen table, Marcel poured *pastis* for everyone who wanted it. As soon as it was drunk, the first course of *charcuterie*, homemade, of course, was served. Thick slices of *jambon cru* and *saucisson* were stacked on platters, and jars of juniper-and-rosemary-scented *pâté* were set out, along with *baguettes* and bottles of red wine filled by Marcel from the vat he kept in his *cave*. We all helped ourselves to the platters and bottles as they passed among us. The second course was invariably pasta, a different shape and size each day, dressed with a meat sauce made from the previous day's leftovers and tomato sauce, a practice I readily adapted to my own kitchen. The pasta was served with *fromage rouge* sprin- 59 kled over the top, a dry orange cheese sealed in red wax that was far less expensive than Parmesan. Marie wouldn't let anyone off with just one helping. "*Servez-vous! Servez-vous!* Have more, please, that's not enough. Eat more," she would say, pushing the bowls and platters toward us. "Go on, go on, serve yourself."

It was hard to resist Marie's attention and even harder to resist the food. You would think that *pâté*, cured ham and sausages, bread, olives, and two healthy servings of pasta would be enough, even for strong men and women in their prime. But no. Marie wanted to be sure no one left hungry and that no one thought she was cheap. She didn't ever want it said that you don't get enough to eat at her house. *Charcuterie* and pasta were only the prelude.

Other farmers' kitchens were rumored to be stingy with the lunches they served to their workers, keeping the good food for *le patron* and his friends. Not at Marie's house. The pasta was fol- lowed by platters heavy with braised rabbit, chicken, or guinea fowl, all raised in the cages and pens in the open barns below the kitchen. They were seasoned with mushrooms she and Marcel had collected and dried the previous fall, and with wild thyme and rosemary and a little dried orange peel. Sautéed zucchini, stuffed tomatoes and eggplant, and freshly dug potatoes accom- panied the meat dish. And always more wine and bread. I usually tried to pass up seconds of the *charcuterie* and pasta in order to have room for the main dish and the vegetables. A salad made from garden-picked greens or maybe wild dandelions came next, the vinaigrette heavy with garlic, and then a platter of cheese. The cheese was always followed by melons, because Marcel was, and still is, a notable melon grower, and grape harvest and melon season coincided.

Toward the end of every meal, Marcel would get up from the table, go down to the *cave*, and bring up four or five melons of different kinds, which he put on the table before sitting down again. Next, he would carefully select one melon and cut a slice from it, scraping the seeds directly onto his plate and cutting the flesh away from the crescent of the skin. Everyone waited. If he pronounced it good, and he usually did with a "Mmhupm," the melon was cut up and passed around on a platter. If not, it went into the bucket to be fed to the pig and chickens. This ritual continued until no one could eat another bite of melon. Finally, Marie made coffee, and then it was time for us to walk back into the vineyards, pick up our buckets, and return to cutting grapes—an astonishing feat after such a meal. But since Marie was well known as one of the best—if not the best—cooks around, people would rather be lethargic in the field than give up ten days at her table.

In the old days on the farms, before World War II, five meals a day were served to the workers, starting at dawn with bread, olive oil or thin slices of lard, maybe jam, and wine or hot coffee, followed by a morning *casse-croûte* of more bread and sausage or *pâté*. Then came a large lunch, and a late-afternoon or early-evening snack similar to the morning one. The day ended well after nightfall with a final meal of soup, vegetables, more bread and wine, and maybe fruit. I can't imagine what five meals a day would have been like at Marie and Marcel's.

Over the more than thirty years that Marie and Marcel have been my friends, I've shared many meals with them and learned many things, among them how to slaughter, dress, and preserve a pig. Donald and I were invited to help when it was their turn for the traveling butcher to come to their house for the *jour du cochon*.

It was still dark when Donald went up the road to help Marcel and the other men build the fire and get the equipment ready. By the time I arrived at the farmhouse courtyard an hour or so later with Ethel and her baby brother, Oliver, steam was rising from the water in the metal oil drum, and smoke from burning grapevines and oak scented the air. A wide plank rested on top of two trestles next to the drum of boiling water. Everyone was bundled up with thick wool scarves and knit hats pulled down over their ears. They spoke quietly, not wanting to upset the pig. They understood that an agitated animal would not bleed well, and if it didn't bleed well, the meat would be tainted, the hams wouldn't cure, and it would be a big loss to the family.

When M. Benedict arrived about half an hour later than scheduled, it was evident he had already had a few shots of *eau-de-vie* from the bottle he pulled out of the truck. Dressed in a heavy white apron, he was short and stocky, with big, red meaty hands and a round red face—the stereotype of a local country butcher. By this time, Ethel had gone to play dolls in a back bedroom with Marie and Marcel's daughter, Aileen, and Oliver was in the kitchen upstairs with Marie's mother watching him. Everyone else was in the courtyard waiting for the ritual slaughter to begin.

M. Benedict shook hands with each of us and then asked, "Glasses?" Marcel had already brought glasses down from the kitchen. The butcher filled them with the homemade, fiery, unaged *eau-de-vie*. We raised our glasses in silence, then drank to the pig in one long swallow. It went down like liquid fire, burning and warming all the way to the bottom of my stomach.

I kept back, out of the way, and watched while M. Benedict directed the men. "You, over there. Throw this rope through the hook," he said, indicating a triangle with sharp hooks on each end. "That's it. No, no a little tighter. Good, good. That's it."

When all was ready, including Marie with a deep yellow plastic basin holding a little wine vinegar, the men became quiet. *La mise à mort*, the killing of the pig, was still steeped in superstition, and the ritual was to be accomplished according to longtime custom. It was important that the pig be treated with respect at its moment of death, a practice reminiscent of old sacrificial rites, because it would be providing the family with food throughout the year. Cooing noises by Marcel and the butcher gently coaxed the pig to come out of his house. The butcher hit him between the eyes with a hammer, and four men, Donald among them, gripped his limbs while the butcher quickly looped a block and tackle over his rear feet and hoisted him up. Once he was secure—it took only seconds—the butcher carefully sank a knife deep into his throat, cutting the jugular vein. The men held the jerking pig as steady as they could while Marie caught the fountain of pumping blood in her yellow basin, stirring it constantly with a wooden spoon so the blood wouldn't coagulate, until no more blood came.

It all happened so quickly and with such swift, sure movements that I barely had time to register the emotion I felt at the passage from life to death. At one moment the pig was a living, breathing, heaving animal, one I had known for the last year as I helped Marie feed him, and in the next moment he was an inanimate object, ready to become food. With the release of blood, I saw his life slowly leaving and his eyes beginning to fade. My heart was pounding and I turned my head. When I looked back moments later, it was over and the transition from life to death completed. It was time to begin the transformation of the pig into *pâté*, sausages, and hams.

Marie left the courtyard and headed upstairs to the kitchen, and I followed. Oliver was sleeping quietly in a nearby bedroom, so I joined Marie and three or four other women, including Marie's mother, in her sixties then, a beautiful Calabrian with pure white hair and the profile of a Roman emperor. "Here. Start sautéing these," Marie said, handing me a cotton sack full of minced onions. I chopped them last night, but they need to cook now in the *saindoux*." *Saindoux*, I learned, was the very fine, delicate fat surrounding the pork kidneys. Once rendered, it was stored and then used for certain sautés and, most importantly, for making pastry crusts, as is rendered back fat. You can still buy *saindoux* at some butcher shops, but none of my French neighbors render their own fat anymore, not even Marie.

Someone came over to the stove to help me hoist the five pounds of onions into pans of melted fat, and we stirred them until they were just beginning to color. Then we put them into a big pot on the table and stirred in the blood. Marie was pounding fennel seeds, coarse salt, and peppercorns together in a mortar. "Not everyone uses wild fennel, but we do." She rubbed some fennel seeds between her fingers and smelled them before passing them to me. "It's better than garden fennel. More flavor. I cut bunches of the wild fennel stalks in the fall and keep them in the *cave*." She added a little nutmeg and allspice, and then stirred the mix into the blood and onions.

"Marie!" shouted Marcel, pounding up the stairs. "Where's the salt?"

"Downstairs!" At first, I had been startled by how much Marie and Marcel shouted at each other, but I finally figured out that it was how they communicated. I followed him a few minutes later to see what was going on in the courtyard. Marcel was downstairs in the large vaulted room, the same room that a few years later would be my kitchen, setting up a low wooden box on a table.

The pig, now most of it scraped smooth, was the palest pink. Donald was ladling a panful of boiling water over the last bristle-covered leg while someone else scraped it. I stayed to watch as the animal was hoisted up and its hocks pierced by the hooks hanging above the courtyard arch. As the butcher made a clean slice down the belly, a torrent of steaming intestines spilled into the big basin held by one of the men, exposing the lungs and heart. It was a primeval scene as the men worked in unison, each understanding the task at hand: pulling on the intestines, cutting in exactly the right place to release them from the stomach wall, cutting again at the bunghole, gently gathering the rest of the fat around the kidneys and putting it into a bowl, cutting out the kidneys and then the liver, and placing them, still steaming, in another bowl.

"Be careful," someone warned Donald. "Don't cut into the gallbladder. It's full of bitterness and will spoil the liver if it gets on it." The morning mist had begun to clear, and the sky showed pale blue as the men finished removing the innards.

I went back upstairs to help the women, and soon parts of the pig began arriving. The onion and blood mixture I had left behind was now snugly packed into casings, and the sausages had been pricked and were poaching in big pots of simmering water. "This one's ready," said Marie's mother, called Mémé Schiffino by almost everyone, who was standing next to the poaching pots. "Take it away," she directed, as she lifted a whole row of sausages out of the pot, where they had hung from strings tied to a willow branch balanced across the rim. Marie's cousin, Bernadette, took the branch from Mémé Schiffino and fastened it onto rope strung around the perimeter of the kitchen. Soon the kitchen was festooned with dangling sausages, and the women were hard at work chopping meat and fat for *pâté*. Oliver was crying to be fed, so I simply watched the process while I nursed him. At the same time, potatoes were being boiled for lunch, and a loin, well rubbed with garlic and sage, the traditional seasonings for pork, was roasting in the oven. Just before noon we were done with the chopping, a pan was on the stove ready for frying up the *boudin*, a salad was made and sitting on the sideboard, the table was set, and I, for one, was exhausted.

65

The men started to come in, and Ethel and Aileen joined us. Oliver had contentedly gone back to sleep in the bedroom. Fifteen minutes later, at exactly noon, we were all sitting at the table as Marcel sliced the traditional cured sausage reserved from the previous year's *fête du cochon*. Copious amounts of wine were poured and bread was passed while Marie tended to the *boudin* sizzling behind us on the stove top. Soon the table was laden with a heaping platter of the crispy, reddish brown *boudin*, bowls of mashed potatoes, and warm applesauce. Starving after our hard morning's work, we quickly devoured the first course. Next came the roast, more vegetables, the salad, cheese, an apple tart that one of Marcel's cousins had made, and, thank goodness, coffee. Then, it was back to work, with the men spending the rest of the afternoon butchering part of the pig and getting it ready for salting, and the women preparing *caillettes*.

My first encounter with *caillettes* had been just outside Arles late one afternoon when I was a student in Aix-en-Provence. Donald and I were with two friends visiting from Germany. We were hungry, but it was too early for a restaurant and too late for a sandwich at a *café*. As we drove through a village, we spotted a *boucherie-charcuterie* and pulled up in front with the idea of buying a few slices of ham. Once inside, I spotted a tray of richly browned, ready-to-eat hamburger patties, which I thought looked absolutely delicious and quite substantial. I could hardly wait. I bought two, and once we were back in the car, I broke them in half and passed them out. What a shock! At first bite, I knew I had made a terrible mistake. They were dense, not crumbly like hamburger, with a strong liver taste and tiny squares of fat, all heavily seasoned with garlic. And there was a bit of something green as well.

I didn't know then that I was sampling part of the culinary patrimony of Provence, one that goes back with certainty to the 1800s and perhaps, in an earlier version, to the 1600s. The rounds, about the size of a hamburger, but shaped more like a ball than a patty, are made from cubes of liver and fat, and occasionally spinach or chard, and then seasoned with salt, pepper, garlic, and spices. Sometimes the preparation is marinated in wine, and sometimes an egg is added. Each round, or *petit ballot*, is then topped with a sprig of sage; wrapped in a square of *crépine*, the lacy caul fat that covers the stomach; and baked for about half an hour in a medium-hot oven. Old recipes indicate that the throat meat of the pig, sometimes called pork sweetbreads because the throat is where sweetbreads are located in a bovine, was used in combination with the liver. Although *caillettes* appear to have originated as humble family fare, the famous Curnonsky includes them in his classic *Le trésor gastronomique de France* as a regional specialty. They are found outside Provence, but are nevertheless considered a *charcuterie* typical of the region. The most illustrious of the Provençal *caillettes* are said to come from the Var, the *département*, or province, where we were living, and are sometimes called *caillettes varoises*. Not surprisingly, different villages each have their own way of preparing them.

In Cotignac, where Marie's family settled after leaving Calabria in 1946, the *caillettes* are made with the kidneys and lungs as well as the liver, and that was how we made ours that day in Marie's kitchen. Once they were done, we put them on platters to cool, and Bernadette spoke up, "Save the *jus*, too. Don't pour that out."

67

She then turned to me. "In the old days the *jus* was a special treat. You can see how the fat has melted, and when we were children we would grill pieces of bread in the fireplace to soak up the *jus*." She tore off several pieces of bread from a leftover *baguette*. "Here, try this."

She dipped a piece into the juices and handed it to me. "Ethel, Aileen, *venez ici!*" she cried, calling the girls from the back bedroom where they were playing, and handed them each a piece of bread. "Go on, dip it in." She tilted the baking dish toward them. *"Non! Je veux pas!"* Aileen, at three years old, knew her own mind, and clearly wasn't having any. It wasn't until she was a young woman that she became as appreciative of her mother's cooking as everyone else was, and there are still a number of things she won't eat. Among them is her grandmother's chocolate cake made with pig's blood, which I can attest tastes wonderful, though I can understand how others might be reluctant to eat it again once they know why it is so moist. Ethel, on the other hand, took a big dip of the warm *jus* and smacked her lips. I don't think she could be enticed so easily today, but when she was little she would usually eat anything as long as it was good. The hot *jus* was delicious, richly flavored with garlic and seasonings and tasting faintly of liver.

J.-B. Reboul's classic *La cuisinière provençale*, a cookbook first published in the 1900s in Marseilles, includes a recipe titled *Crépinettes de foie à la villageoise ou gayettes. Gayettes* is another spelling of *caillettes*. You begin by putting the cubed fat in one plate, the cubed pork liver in another, and then seasoning the fat well with a mixture of salt, pepper, spices, and three or four cloves of minced garlic. Next, you lay squares of caul fat on the table and layer each one first with cubed fat and then with cubed liver. You repeat this twice. The caul fat is tied with string to make a packet, and the *caillettes* are baked in a *gratin* dish for about half an hour. They are typically served cold and sliced, like *pâté*.

A fine *caillette* is still much appreciated at local dinner tables, but since few people make their own anymore, it is necessary to find a *charcutier* who not only makes his own, but also makes good ones. M. Desmoulins is just such a butcher. He no longer has his fixed shop in Aups, a neighboring village, preferring instead to keep only his traveling shop. It is a special van outfitted with an upper panel that folds up to reveal a long, refrigerated, glass-protected counter filled with house-made *charcuterie*, roasts, shanks, and various cuts of pork, beef, and lamb. A large selection of sharp knives and cutting boards is visible and the interior is gleaming, bright white. M. Desmoulins stands behind the counter ready to serve, take orders, chat, and answer questions. I have often bought *caillettes* from him when he makes his Sunday morning stop in front of the *bar-tabac* in Tavernes, the closest village to my house, about five minutes away by the back road, and have served them to local guests who say, "Ah, are these from Desmoulins? They look like it." The moment I confirm their suspicions, they take an ample slice.

While we were making our *caillettes* at Marie's that afternoon and sampling the *jus*, the men were setting up the *saloir*, the wooden box with sloping sides that I had seen earlier downstairs. The *saloir* is where meats are packed in salt for curing, and Marcel's was an old one. I could see the hand-carved wooden pegs holding it together as I watched him pour a thick layer of coarse salt into the bottom. He laid the fresh hams and pork bellies on top of the salt, but before covering them with more salt, he pushed down around the ham joints with his thumb, packing the area with salt. A trickle of clear pink fluid came out. "Don't want any blood in there. Spoils the meat. Do this twice a day. Turn the meat too. Have to." He poured on more salt until the meats were buried. According to tradition, I shouldn't have been in the salting room that day because the old lore surrounding the killing and preserving of the pig alleges that the presence of women in the salting room will cause the meat to spoil.

69

Marcel had been orphaned when he was little, his parents felled by a flu epidemic, and he had stopped school at ten, when he was sent to work as a farmhand far from Nice, but he had his own mind about things. He has never been afraid to stand his ground about what he thought was right, in spite of the village hierarchy that once put him and Marie very near the bottom because they were tenant farmers and "foreigners," the latter ascribed to anyone less than second or third generation in the village.

"Best place in the whole village for hams," he said as he looked around the room and smoothed the salt over the meat. "I'll hang and season the legs in thirty days." He indicated the hook in the middle of the vaulted ceiling with an upward jerk of his head. "Stays cool here, got air." This time he motioned with his head to his left in the direction of a small, barred window over the old stone sink. It had a piece of screen nailed over it. When the room later became our kitchen, we left the hook in the ceiling but glassed in the window. By that time, the curing of hams in the sixteenth-century vaulted room had passed into memory, with only Marcel and a few others remembering the days when they killed pigs and hung hams there to provision the family.

Although thirty years ago preserving parts of the pig was a necessity of rural life, the *jour du cochon* has disappeared from most of the villages. *Charcuterie*, however, still figures large in the appetites and traditions of Provence. Every village has a butcher or two, and the larger towns and cities have many. Locals know which day which butcher makes *boudin maison*, which one makes the best *pâté de campagne*, and which one sells the most tender *jambon*. The measure of the importance of *charcuterie* in the culinary life of Provence, and of all of France, can be measured by the amount of shelf space devoted to it in supermarkets. You can even buy multiple versions of *boudin* in supermarkets: large fat ones, slim or plump medium ones, whole long rolls, single links. There is even an *apéritif* version spiced with seasonings from the Antilles that is grilled and served speared on a toothpick with before-dinner drinks. The kinds of *pâtés*, certainly from pork, but from other meats as well, seem countless, as do the dried and fresh sausages and pickled preparations.

Anne, my longtime friend from my student days in Aix-en-Provence, who helps me now with my cooking classes, loves *museau de porc*. "It reminds me of being a little girl in Marseille, when my father, who was a schoolteacher like my mother, would bring us home a treat on his way back from school. We'd all gather around the kitchen table and he'd cut slices of fresh *baguette* for us and make *museau* sandwiches," she once told me, passing me a little plastic box of thinly sliced pickled snout, onions, and *cornichons* as we sat at a *café* on market day in Salernes. "I got this across the street." She indicated a small butcher shop with red tile trimming its windows. "They make it themselves, but only once in a while. I always look for it." She picked a slice out of the box and began to eat it. "I eat too much bread," she laughed, "so now, just the *museau* on its own, not a sandwich." We picked the box clean, then washed the impromptu snack down with a *café crème* for me, tomato juice for Anne.

Another *charcuterie* item, *saucisson d'Arles*, is, like the *caillette*, particular to Provence, but now is famous all over France. As with any special food or dish with a history, many legends surround it, but we do know that the rose-hued sausage of Arles has been made since the seventeenth century. Traditional wisdom varies on just how it was first prepared. Some say that the original sausage was donkey meat, others that it was a mixture of pork, beef, and donkey or horse meat, and still others that it was made from the meat of the wild cattle of the Camargue. Not one of these theories has been confirmed. What is known is that today the sausage is made from lean pork, lean beef, and pork fat, all chopped separately. Then they are mixed together with wine, herbs, salt, and pepper and stuffed into large beef intestines, which are twisted into individual sausages and dried for three to six weeks under controlled conditions.

71

....

Following that wonderful day at Marcel and Marie's we never participated in the *jour du cochon* again in France. We left our life in Provence just months later, after first buying the apartment adjacent to theirs, the one that included the vaulted room, plus an assortment of barns, outbuildings, and a bit of land. Donald's father had died suddenly, and we decided to return to California. Donald left almost immediately, taking Oliver, who was only six months old, and Ethel with him.

I stayed on to sell the animals and pack up our belongings. I sold Lucretia to a farmer in the neighboring *département*, Alpes-de-Haute-Provence. She was quite pregnant then, and he was delighted to have her. I cried as she struggled up the ramp into the back of his van, both for the loss of our pig and for the loss of our hopes for a quiet, civilized life in rural Provence. By then, M. Gos had gotten rid of most of his pigs, keeping only a few. "I'd like to take her," he said, "but I'm getting too old." When we returned to France three years later, he was dead, and his last pig gone. His widow hugged us, her black eyes bright with tears, when we went to see her, and she brought out a bag of candy for Ethel and Oliver.

Marcel and a few others continued to buy young pigs and raise them for provisions for another five or six years, but times were changing. As grapevines were pulled out and the land replanted with wheat, which was mechanically harvested, the need for farmworkers, and thus the need to feed them, diminished. Supermarkets were built in neighboring villages, people bought freezers, and the old customs began to be extraneous. Even so, Marcel still buys a part of a pig, and though he is not supposed to eat *charcuterie,* and certainly is not supposed to spread his bread with lard, he and Marie make up a few provisions.

Over the years Donald and I re-created the *jour du cochon* in California, buying pigs from local 4-H or Future Farmers of America projects, or from the few farmers who raised and sold them, mainly to a Spanish and Hispanic clientele. We made *boudin, pâté,* and *caillette,* just as we had learned from Marie and Marcel, and froze the fresh hams since we didn't have the correct conditions for curing them properly.

Even though he had never participated in one before, my second husband, Jim, and I had a *jour du cochon,* too. Adele and Pascal, neighbors from Provence, were living near us in California, where Adèle was a Fulbright exchange teacher for a year, and they often spent the weekends with us. One winter weekend when Adèle and Pascal were planning to visit, we arranged for a retired butcher friend to help us do a *jour de cochon*. The butcher's wife and other friends came to assist and share the feast, which lasted well into the late afternoon, and it is the taste of warm, juicy *caillettes* that everyone still remembers most from that day.

73

Porc à l'ancienne avec moutarde et câpres

BRAISED PORK SHOULDER WITH MUSTARD AND CAPERS

I love this dish on a cold winter night, served very hot with a creamy potato *gratin* and ample bread and red wine. Cheeks are the very best cut for this dish, but shoulder works just as well. Both cuts are meaty and tough, full of the connective tissue that, with long, slow oven-cooking, dissolves to create the thick sauce and spoon-tender meat that gives the dish its character.

Preheat an oven to 325 degrees F. Cut a 2½- to 3-pound piece of pork shoulder, also called picnic ham, into large pieces about 2 inches thick. Dry the pieces well and season them with a goodly amount of coarse sea salt and freshly ground black pepper. Put a thick slice of lard in a Dutch oven and render it over low heat. You should have enough fat to cover the bottom of the pot about ¼ inch deep. If you don't have lard, use a combination of extra-virgin olive oil and butter.

When the fat has melted, increase the heat and brown the meat, a few pieces at a time, on all sides. As they brown to your satisfaction, remove them to a bowl and continue until all the meat is browned.

To the fat in the pan, add a handful or two of chopped onion, the same amount of chopped leeks, using both white and pale green parts, and two carrots cut into three or four pieces. Sauté for a few minutes until the edges of the onion start to brown.

Pour in about a third of a bottle of dry red wine—I like to use an inexpensive one from the Rhône or elsewhere in southern France—and scrape up any brown bits clinging to the bottom of the pan. Return the meat and the juices that have collected in the bowl to the pan, then stir in a teaspoonful of minced fresh rosemary.

Cover the pan and put it in the oven. Cook the pork, stirring from time to time, until it is tender enough to cut with a spoon and some of the pieces are slightly ragged. This will take about 3 hours.

To finish, remove the carrots and discard them, because they have given up their flavor to the sauce. Stir in a heaping tablespoon of Dijon mustard—a *fines herbes* version is especially good in this dish—and an equally large tablespoon of capers, plus a little more fresh rosemary. Serve the pork very hot. Leftovers make a sumptuous sauce for pasta.

SERVES 4 TO 6

FUNGAL OBSESSIONS

Georgette's mushroom primer. Foraging success. The pas mals
and the pas bons. *M. Capretti's truffle.*

When I had been in Provence barely a year, our new neighbor, Georgette, initiated me into *la cueillette des champignons*, the seasonal gathering of wild mushrooms.

"Do you know what these are?" She held out her basket filled with a tangled heap of orangish stems and caps mixed with pine needles, decaying oak leaves, and dirt as I set our outdoor table for lunch.

"Well, they look like mushrooms." The concave caps showed concentric, almost iridescent orange rings and were glazed a copperish green. "But not like any I've ever seen before." I hesitated before touching one. "Where did you get them?"

"Ah ha, I thought so," she said, ignoring my question. "You don't have these in the United States, I bet. They are special to here, to Provence. They're called *sanguins, sanguin* for the blood-red color of their juice." She broke an edge off one of the caps. The exposed meat seeped crimson.

"They're in our forests now. In the pine and oak. *Ils sont très bons à manger*. I'll show you." She put her basket down and firmly took my arm, guiding me toward her woodpile. "Here," she said, handing me an armload of grapevine prunings, "take these over to your barbecue."

Barbecue was a generous term for the six bricks we had double-stacked into three sides of a rectangle over the shallow pit Donald and I had dug in a corner of our yard. Here we built small fires, then laid a rack on top to grill sausages or lamb or pork chops, and next, it seemed, mushrooms.

Georgette arranged the prunings. "First we have to clean the mushrooms," she said. I pushed aside the plates I had brought out earlier, and she, Ethel, and I sat down at the table.

"Do you have a little brush?" Georgette asked.

"I don't think so."

"No old toothbrush?"

"No. We're using all our toothbrushes."

"OK," she said, jumping up. "I'll be right back." She headed to her house, which was just the length of our yard and her flagstone terrace away, and returned in minutes with an old toothbrush and a large bowl.

"You have to brush off the dirt and the pine needles," she instructed, as she sat back down. "Watch me." Ethel and I did as we were told, observing as Georgette gently brushed the mushroom caps and gills, making a soft, whishing sound, then used her fingers to remove large pine needles or recalcitrant oak leaves.

"Georgeanne, get a cutting board and a knife from your kitchen."

I obeyed.

"Now, trim the stem end of each one. Just a little," she said.

I started cutting the ends of the cleaned mushrooms. The stems were hollow and bled less than the caps when cut.

"I want to try," Ethel said to Georgette. Georgette smiled, handed my daughter the brush, and huddled with her over a mushroom. Georgette praised Ethel as she successfully brushed several pine needles and a little dirt from a mushroom.

"You finish these." She pushed the remaining mushrooms toward her, then turned to me. "I found these along the path that goes to the *roc de bidau*. Usually the hunters get there first, but not this time." She laughed, unfastening the clip that held back her reddish brown hair, shaking it loose, and then reclipping it.

The *roc de bidau* was one of my favorite places, a big stone outcropping that stood guard over our little valley. Footpaths led up and through the forests to it, and once there, standing on top of the rock itself, I could see north to the beginning of the Alps and across the collection of cultivated valleys, hills, and forests that made up our immediate landscape. One time Donald, Ethel, and I packed a picnic and went to the top of the rock, with Tune, our dog, following us as always. There we spread out a cloth for our ham sandwiches, fresh goat cheese, and apples.

"Besides, there was so much rain in September," Georgette continued, unaware of my reverie, "that we are going to have a very, very good year for mushrooms. Rain in September means mushrooms in October. The *sanguins* are best grilled, which is what we are going to do. You can also pickle them or dry them. Some people use them in *omelettes*, but *chanterelles* are much better for that. The best for drying are the *cèpes*, but they're harder to find around here. If you go to the forests above

Bauduen and Aiguines you'll find them. They like the higher altitudes. Certain people know all the secret places. And as for the *chanterelles* . . . ahh, *superbe!*

"You know the forest where you take your goats? There will be lots of mushrooms to gather there, I am sure. Look near the water for the *chanterelles*." Her slender fingers with their blunt-cut nails and single gold band never rested, cleaning as fast as she was talking.

More than the seasonal gathering of wild edibles, *la cueillette* in Provence is a social and cultural ritual that is repeated annually, marking the food calendar of urban as well as rural inhabitants. To participate in *la cueillette* is to begin to understand that the food in Provence is inextricably linked to rural traditions that even the most die-hard urbanites value as part of their cultural consciousness and gastronomic patrimony. This is one of the things I most value about life in Provence, and one that seems never to change, no matter how many years pass.

I had always loved mushrooms, and in the Southern California of the 1950s and 1960s that I had left behind, fresh, white button mushrooms were considered exotic. The rich world of edible wild mushrooms that was to become an integral part of both my French life and my California life lay ahead.

"A *chanterelle* looks like a small trumpet, and is a beautiful, pale apricot color," Georgette explained. "One side of the trumpet is longer and larger than the other. Underneath, the gills are wavy, not straight. You look for those when you are out with your goats."

I've learned so much from Georgette over the years, beginning with the mushrooms. She was atypical of the local women I met those first two years we lived in Provence, being well educated, from a politically active family, a left-wing artist, and a former schoolteacher. However, she knew and respected the ways and traditions of the region as much as any farmer's wife. Having grown up during the war years, she was naturally frugal, a remnant of a time of scarcity and uncertainty, and she valued every bit of food that she prepared.

Almost immediately after we moved into the small house that we rented from Georgette and her husband, Denys, she took me in hand and gently taught me the foodways of rural Provence, and through me, the next generation, Ethel. I felt there was a strong personal element for her as well: She didn't want a neighbor, especially a foreign one, who wasn't properly informed about the local life and traditions, most of which seemed to revolve around food—the ways to grow and harvest, to gather and clean, to cook and preserve, and to celebrate. In me she had found a willing student.

"When you're in the forest I also want you to look for *sanguins*. You know what those look like now. Search under the oak and pine trees. You may find *cèpes* there too. I don't suppose you know what those look like either." She didn't even pause before continuing.

"They have very round caps. They can be any size. Underneath they have no gills, just sponge, creamy white sponge. Don't be fooled by the ones with yellow sponge. Those are no good. Mushroom hunting is part of life here," she declared as she inspected Ethel's work, "and we look forward to gathering them every fall. Now you can too!"

I was intrigued but naturally apprehensive in spite of Georgette's air of authority on the desirability of cooking and eating wild mushrooms. When I was a child, my mother had

severely warned me about the white and tan fungi that periodically forced their way up through the grass in the front yard of
our Southern California home, saying we didn't know how to
tell an edible mushroom from a poisonous toadstool, and even
touching a poisonous one would give us warts. In her estimation,
such things were best left for leprechauns and fairies, but that
didn't stop her from making *coq au vin* with the expensive fresh
mushrooms she had to buy at the high-end greengrocer in town.

As they cooked over the grape prunings, the *sanguins* released
the scent of warming garlic, hissing as Georgette brushed them
with olive oil, which dripped onto the hot coals. With a toothpick and a quiver of misgiving, my mother's warnings singing in
my head, I speared one of the golden brown quarters that my
mushroom mentor had put on a platter. Firm to the bite, with
a slightly rough texture, the morsel tasted earthy, with a hint
of pine, and of garlic and olive oil. As I watched Ethel eat the
first mushroom, then take a second, I thought how different her
childhood experiences were going to be from mine.

Donald arrived just as the grilling was done and we gathered
around, continuing to eat straight off the grill, washing the *sanguins* down with the *rosé* Denys had brought over when he came
home from school for lunch.

"So. What do you think?" Georgette licked her fingers and
answered her own question. "Good, aren't they?"

"Yes." I agreed, licking the last of the olive oil from my lips.

....

After lunch, Ethel and I went back to the goat barn with Donald.
I gave the goats the leftover dried bread I had been storing up for
them, and then the three of us went into the forest to look for

mushrooms. We left the goats inside their enclosure, knowing that if we took them into the forest we'd spend most of our time watching out for them instead of searching for fungi. I carried a basket and a knife. Georgette had explained that one should always cut, never pull, them from the ground to leave spore behind for the next season. That way, she said, the mushrooms will continue to regenerate.

I wandered through the forest, cutting in and out of the sharp prickly juniper bushes and dodging the odd low-hanging pine branches, and kept my eyes to the forest floor. It was dark under the trees, and the earth was damp from the rains, smelling as if it had just been turned, strong and peatlike, almost stinging the nostrils. I sensed the aroma of fungi. As soon as I found my first mushrooms, a cluster of *sanguins* pushing up the layers of molding leaves, I knew that I was hooked. It was like a treasure hunt, but the prizes weren't the Woolworth trinkets of my childhood. They were wild mushrooms. I was in a forest in France, gathering my own food—and I was succeeding.

I have a fading photograph of me taken that day. I'm wearing an orange wool maternity tunic with a purple turtleneck underneath, my hair pulled back at the nape of my neck in a ponytail, with a huge smile, hovering over my finds.

Some of the mushrooms I found that day grew closely together in clusters, while others stood in solitary splendor. A shockingly huge one had a bulbous yellow, red-veined stem and a spongy undercap that bruised deep indigo when I touched it. I was certain that anything so sinister looking had to be poisonous, so I kept it separate from my other finds.

By the time Donald insisted we head back, my basket was filled with mushrooms in shades of blue, gray, purple, tan, gold, white, and brown. I had picked at least a few of everything I had found, just in case they were edible, leaving behind those that were obviously too old and were rotting or slimy.

As soon as we got home I went next door to Georgette's and showed her my collection. She quickly sorted through them, tossing aside most of them, leaving a dozen or so behind. I had indeed found *chanterelles*. *"Pas mal, pas mal,"* she said as she turned each of the four over and over in her hand, inspecting them before going on to the next. "These are *cèpes*, the very best, and you have *sanguins* too. Good, good for you. Bravo." Then she turned to the discards, telling me none were deadly, but none were good to eat either.

"How about this one?" I pulled the big red one out of my bag.

"Oh, *c'est l'horreur! Ce n'est pas bon du tout, du tout.* It's not good at all, not at all! It's *le bolet de satan!* It will make you very, very sick if you eat it. Go wash your hands right away. At least you didn't keep it with the others!" She smiled as I nodded knowingly.

"You knew it was bad, didn't you?" I thought she seemed proud of me. "Here, take your mushrooms, and clean them like I showed you. Make an *omelette* with these," she said, indicating the *chanterelles*, "and a sauce for a beefsteak with the rest."

Donald lit a fire in our kitchen's woodstove and we all set about the task of cleaning our mushrooms. I put out some bread, olive oil, and fresh goat cheese for us to snack on because it was already late and we were hungry. I carefully sliced our *chanterelles* into long, perfect sections and sautéed them in olive oil with a few shallots, salt, and pepper. As they cooked, they scented our little kitchen with an unfamiliar aroma, slightly musty and rich.

When they became tender, I poured a half-dozen beaten eggs over them and sprinkled on parsley. I let the bottom of the eggs set, then flipped one half over the other, cooking the *omelette* until it was firm, but still soft in the middle. I quickly made a salad from greens I had picked earlier that day, and we sat down to our first home-cooked meal of gathered wild mushrooms.

The next day I made a *fricassée* with the *cèpes* and *sanguins*, sautéing them together with garlic, onions, and butter until they were lightly browned. I added some white wine to deglaze the pan, and followed that with some fresh curds and a few crushed wild juniper berries to make a sauce. The *cèpes* smelled very different from the *chanterelles*, having more of a woodland perfume aroma. I wanted to serve the sauce over steak, as Georgette suggested, but pasta, topped with some grated *Gruyère,* was a good substitute for the more expensive steak.

I went mushroom hunting almost daily thereafter until the first frosts came in early November and the season ended. We ate wild mushrooms in some form or another almost every day, but my favorites were, and still are, *cèpes* and *chanterelles* braised with rabbit and black olives, and the mixtures of different kinds, whatever the forest yields, simply sautéed in butter, wine, and garlic and heaped on top of grilled toasts or added to salads.

I became such a successful hunter-gatherer, as did Ethel and Donald, that we had to dry some of our *sanguins* or watch them spoil. We simply couldn't eat them all fresh in the quantities we found. Marie, another neighbor, showed Ethel and me how to dry them. After we cleaned the mushrooms we sliced them and threaded the slices onto long strings with a needle. We proudly hung festoons of mushrooms on rafters near the woodstove to dry before we packed them into tins for storage.

....

The passion for mushroom hunting that is so evident in Provence is rooted partially in the collective memory, when *la cueillette* formed an essential element in the diet of rural families, and partially in the love of hunting and gathering, which connects the Provençaux to nature and the land, even if they live in cities.

In the old days, knowing the special spots where mushrooms could be found provided a sense of food security, not unlike having rabbits in hutches or vegetables in the garden, along with a bit of a smug triumph when trumping a neighbor or relative with an especially large or laudable haul. If the sense of food security is no longer a driving force behind the hunt, the sense of triumph and the meal to come still are.

This was brought home to me not long ago when a friend's very wealthy Parisian brother and his wife were visiting, and they all went up to the hills near Aiguines, above the Lac de Sainte-Croix, to hunt mushrooms.

"Look at this! I hear you like to go mushroom hunting, so we just had to come and show you what we found," the wife said, dropping her Armani coat on my chair. She put a large basket filled with fungi on my table and began pulling out the best specimens first, waving big, fat, perfect *cèpes* and handfuls of golden *chanterelles* under my nose, then pulling them back. As she dug through her basket, big diamond and gold rings glittered on her fingers, incongruous with the dirt beneath her nails and smudged on her hands.

I asked her, half joking, "And which ones are for me?"

"Mais non, Madame," she responded with a shocked air. "Not for you at all. These are mine. We will cook them tonight, first a *brouillé,* then tomorrow a *fricassée,* I think."

"Quite a prize, for the Parisienne, don't you think? My grandmother, after all, came from a farm in the Languedoc, and I know a few things about *la cueillette*, right, *chérie*?" She turned to her husband as she repacked all her prizes into her basket and put her coat back on.

"Well, ah, thank you for your visit. You certainly had a very good day. Beautiful mushrooms, and *bon appétit*." I closed the door behind them, somewhat dismayed that the visit had simply been to gloat, not to share. Just one of those fat *cèpes* or two or three of the *chanterelles* would have been just right to go with my dinner. Instead, I studded the pork loin I had bought that morning with garlic, and ground some fresh bay leaf and juniper together to rub on it. The potatoes I cooked with the pork were newly dug, and I sautéed some spinach before adding a little *crème fraîche*. It was a delicious meal, but those mushrooms would have made a good pan sauce for the pork.

....

While mushroom hunting is an intense, recreational pastime in Provence, it is also big business, as it is elsewhere in France, with thousands of tons being gathered and sold every year. Many people, especially in the still relatively unpopulated, forested areas of Haute-Provence, supplement their income by gathering mushrooms and selling them to brokers, who in turn sell them to large firms from where they make their way to markets throughout the world, to be sold fresh, or to be dried, canned, or otherwise preserved. It is not a small thing.

Recognizing the economic importance to the *commune*, or administrative district, and the role that mushrooms still play in the food of rural life, communal forests especially thick with fungi are posted off-limits to nonlocals: *"Cueillette de champignons inter-dite sauf aux habitants de commune."* This gave our friends Mark and Nina Haag, who lived in the mountains, a slight advantage.

It was at their house that I first experienced *la cueillette* for profit, slightly more than five years after Georgette introduced me to wild mushroom hunting. Mark and Nina, American friends from our early days in Provence, now kept goats and made goat's-milk cheese after buying a small farmhouse and more than sixty hectares of land in the mountains northwest of Nice in the Alpes-Maritimes. Their place was so remote that it was accessible only by narrow footpaths, an hour's climb from the last house in the tiny perched village of La Baume, five kilometers from Annot. Ethel and Oliver loved to visit them, finding their lack of electricity and plumbing exciting, and although I often moaned about the long, steep climb, they scampered ahead through the bracken, eager to see the donkey Mark and Nina kept, and to play with the sheepdogs and goats. This time, we were no more than a couple hundred meters into the forest when we were greeted with a large sign forbidding mushroom collection except for locals. We saw several more postings as we made our way higher and deeper into the forest, following the rutted footpath as it cut through the hardwood forest.

Before the countryside was decimated by two world wars and a pandemic flu, dozens of farmhouses and tiny hamlets stretched across the mountains, all linked by footpaths, shared work, and marriages. By the time Mark and Nina bought their farmhouse in 1975, the forests and weather had reclaimed most of the abandoned stone structures, including many terraces built on the sloping hillsides to grow chestnut trees, once an important crop for the inhabitants.

We arrived, me out of breath, hot, and sweaty, to find
Mark waiting for us. He wanted to hurry, telling us that the
mushroom-hunting season was early this year and Nina was
already out. I leapt at the opportunity. I hadn't been mushroom
hunting in Provence since the fall Oliver was born. Now, he was
five years old and intrigued by the idea of hunting mushrooms.
Ethel informed him she knew all about it.

89

After a drink of cold water drawn from their well, we set out,
the dogs following us. I found I wasn't so tired after all and was
excited about looking for mushrooms again. Mark strode across
the pastures he had cut out of the forests, leading us up into the
high chestnut terraces, about a half-hour climb beyond their
house. "It's going to be a great year, just like the last. Nina sold
more than four kilos of *cèpes* last year. This year she's already sold
about fifty kilos and the season's just started."

"Where does she sell them?" I tried to imagine how she
would have gone about transporting such heavy loads of mushrooms down the twisting path to the village.

"There're brokers who come to Annot. There's always one or
more around. Pay cash too. The *cèpes* brought in enough money
last year to buy two donkeys and a used Renault."

We stood under the chestnut trees whose thick canopies
cast the molding leaves, moss, and crumbling stone walls in
even darker tones. My nose tickled with the dampness and the
smell of the hidden mushrooms. The dense sponge of decaying
matter sighed and gave way as I stepped across it, head down,
looking for fungi.

"Look. There're some right there." Mark strode toward a
swollen hump of leaves. He flipped their mass away with the
stick he was carrying, exposing a cluster of firm, rounded, russet

brown mushroom caps. Oliver knelt down to touch them, Ethel right behind him.

Mark turned to me. "Do you want to cut them?" He handed me his knife.

"Thanks. I have my own knife." I bent down, brushed the remaining leaves aside, and cut through the thick bulbous stems of some of the finest *cèpes* of my mushroom hunting-experience, past or present.

"See," I said to Ethel and Oliver, "you don't want to pull them up because that would take away the spores, the things like little seeds, that make them grow. If you cut them like this"—I handed him the mushrooms, showing him the ends— "more will come back next year and next and probably forever." I was conscious that I was teaching my children what Georgette had taught me, showing them another world and way of life.

"Forever?" Oliver asked, holding the bouquet of mushrooms in his little hands. "Well, at least for a long time," I replied.

"I already know not to pull them up," Ethel said. "I remember from when we used to go in our forest with the goats."

"Can I go look by myself?" Oliver asked, waving a small dry branch around.

"Me, too," said Ethel. "Come on, Oliver, I'll show you."

"Wait," I cried, as they ran off across the broken terraces, "don't pull them up, remember. And don't eat any! Call me or Dad or Mark to bring a knife. And watch out for the stones!"

I barely had time to shout my warnings before Oliver called out, "Mommy, look, we've found some already. Hurry." My two children stood pointing excitedly to the clump of *cèpes* at their feet.

After I cut the fungi, I turned them over. "Look at the underneath part. See how it looks like tan foam or sponge rubber? That means these are *cèpes*. If the tops were brown, but the underneath gills rippling, we wouldn't eat them. Do you understand? Some mushrooms can be very, very dangerous." I didn't think they would take a bite of any, but I wanted to be sure.

Within an hour of wandering through the chestnut terraces, poking through the molding leaves, my basket and Mark's were full of *cèpes*, plus I had a plastic bag of what we determined to be "bad" mushrooms, which we were going to try to identify using Mark's field guide once we got back to the house. Oliver insisted on carrying the bag, holding it gingerly at arm's length, stopping every now and then to open it and look. I think he was fascinated by the idea that he had, right there in his hand, potentially poisonous, even fatal mushrooms, many of which he had found himself.

That evening, before dinner, we sat around the long walnut table Mark had made and, by the light of a kerosene lamp, sorted through Oliver's bag. None of the mushrooms we had found were deadly, but all of them would have made us very, very sick if we had eaten them, which delighted Oliver, who shivered at his brush with poisonous mushrooms. After washing our hands, we cleaned and sliced a couple handfuls of *cèpes*, and Nina added them to the stew of wild boar simmering on the back of the wood-burning stove. As darkness closed in around us, we ate a plate of ham that Mark had salt-cured, with bread that Nina had made in the stone oven built into a covered portico outside the house, and we drank a bottle of red wine, watching the moon rise through the small paned window, casting the slopes below us in a purplish haze. The only sounds were our voices and the gentle bubble from the back of the stove. Soon the small kitchen–living room was filled with the aroma of meat and mushrooms, and Nina brought the stew to the table, ladling it into bowls.

"Our neighbor on the next mountain shot it and gave us this chunk a few days ago. We have to eat it because there is no way to store it," Mark told us as we dipped our bread into the thick sauce. This was my first experience with wild boar, and I was a little apprehensive about eating it, fearing it would be too strong, but it wasn't. It was rich and tender, and the fat slices of *cèpes*, with their earthy perfume, straight from the forest, gathered with our own hands, made a perfect companion for the meat.

After the children had gone to bed, Donald, Mark, and I helped Nina sort, clean, and pack into baskets the *cèpes* she had picked in the forest that day. The next morning we helped her carry them down the mountain, then gave her a ride to Annot to meet the broker.

....

Of the more than seventy mushroom varieties found in and around Provence, the one that is said to cause 95 percent of the several hundred mushroom-related deaths that occur each year during *la cueillette* is the commonly found *Amanita phalloides*. It is part of a family that includes several deadly mushrooms; others that, while not fatal, are poisonous; and, paradoxically, a variety that is ranked as one of the most exquisite tasting of all wild mushrooms, the *Amanita caesarea*.

The amanitas all share certain characteristics: They have a universal veil, a cottonlike membrane that covers the young mushroom completely, causing it to look like an egg as it emerges from the earth. As the mushroom grows, the veil breaks, leaving behind a soft skin resembling an egg shell at the base of the stalk, called a volva. Sometimes the amanitas have a partial veil as well, which looks like a collar around the upper stalk. Unlike the boletus family, with its spongy undercaps, the amanitas have gills. Their cap colors range from white to tan, yellow, gray, and greenish, with the most spectacular being *Amanita muscaria*, which is brilliant red-orange with white, wartlike specks. Its common name is *tue-mouche*, or fly amanita, so-called because it has long been used to stun flies.

The two most infamous of the family are *Amanita phalloides*, the death cap, which has a brown to greenish cap, and *Amanita ocreata*, the destroying angel, which has a white cap that turns brownish buff or variations thereof as it ages. As their names suggest, they are fatal and their poison has no known antidote. The first symptoms, difficulty breathing, dizziness, and aching, don't appear for six to twelve hours and by then the deadly toxin has begun to spread throughout the body, causing violent vomiting, diarrhea, and dehydration. By the third day the victim appears to be improving, but since the toxins cannot be eliminated by the liver, unseen damage is spreading throughout the body's system, and a relapse occurs, with organ breakdown and death by the sixth day. It is a slow, painful death.

Coprinus atramentarius, inky cap or tippler's bane, is perfectly edible and reputedly delicious, except in conjunction with alcohol. The combination can result in light-headedness, increased heart rate, nausea, and vomiting. In severe reactions, hospitalization is required, a misfortune that happened to an acquaintance of mine who was careless about his mushrooms and wound up having his stomach pumped in the emergency room of a hospital in Nice after several *pastis* and a fine inky cap *omelette*, accompanied by a half bottle of Châteauneuf-du-Pape.

Fear of the fatal doesn't seem to dampen the enthusiasm for gathering wild mushrooms. It is a mainstream activity, and the season is eagerly anticipated by everyone. Fall issues of French food and cooking magazines feature mushrooms *à la cueillette* on their covers, and the insides are packed with recipes for cooking the fungi in conjunction with other autumnal foods, such as quince, pears, hard squash, walnuts, and persimmons.

94

Pharmacies take down summer's posters of bronzed beauties touting tanning creams and replace them with botanically accurate renditions of fungi. Often, plaster models of mushrooms are the featured window display. This is both a service and an advertisement of sorts. Pharmacists in France are trained in mycology and as a public service offer free identification of wild mushrooms that are brought to them in a national attempt to educate mushroom enthusiasts and to reduce the number of mishaps that occur from eating toxic mushrooms.

I've never taken mushrooms to a pharmacist myself, but have watched others do so. Once, a youngish man, dressed in an open-necked white shirt, pressed brown pants, and sturdy leather shoes with heavy rubber soles, came into the pharmacy in Barjols where I was waiting for a prescription to be filled and placed a basket of mushrooms on the counter. It's a small pharmacy in a village of fewer than two thousand people, but it's quite modern, with gleaming white walls, bright lighting, and a good stock of medicines and beauty products displayed on sparkling glass shelves and counters. The assistants and the cashier wore crisp white jackets, like the pharmacist.

The damp, primeval smell of mushroom and forest emitted strongly from the basket, the antithesis of the hygienic atmosphere. "There's someone here with mushrooms," called out one of the women in white to the pharmacist working in back. He quickly emerged, rubbing his hands together in anticipation.

"Ah, what have we here?" He reached into the basket and pulled out what I knew was an overripe *pisacane*, the local nickname for a member of the boletus family that is edible, though not very good, and is thought to cause excessive urination and constipation. It is readily identifiable by the darkish yellow sponge or pores on its underside. As it ages, the pores brown, the tops slime, and the stem and body quickly become home to thickets of maggots. *"Pas bon,"* the pharmacist declared, wrinkling his nose and tossing it aside, along with several others of the same type, all in poor condition.

I watched as the pharmacist continued to sort through the basket, tossing aside the *pas bon* and the *trés mauvais* mushrooms, and stacking the ones he declared *bon* and *trés bon* in a neat pile.

"Mmm. Nice." He held up a large, perfectly shaped *Boletus edulis*. *"Cèpes* are delicious. Among the very best. Where did you find this one?"

"Ah, non, Monsieur. I cannot tell you where. My grandmother always told me to keep her mushroom places secret. I have tried hard to remember them. It was a long time ago she took me to the forests with her and showed me where to look."

"Ah, well," laughed the pharmacist, "it never hurts to ask."

I always know mushroom season is beginning when local newspapers such as the *Var-Matin* and *Le Provençal* feature photographs of huge, recently found *cèpes* on their front pages. By the next day, cars are parked in profusion along the roadsides and fill the edges of forest clearings while their occupants forage. The hunt is on. In the open markets and *cafés*, the crossroads of information, everyone is talking about what they have found and when—but never where—they are going hunting, and predicting the length and quality of the season, and local vendors begin displaying their fresh finds.

Whenever I am in Provence in the fall, I join in, hunting almost daily, accepting any invitation to go mushroom hunting, even taking my culinary program students out into the forests.

96

I have limited my personal mushroom gathering to the types that have such a distinct appearance they can't be confused with any other mushroom. I gather only *cèpes, chanterelles, sanguins,* and *pieds-de-mouton,* hedgehog mushrooms, whose spores hang beneath the rough, irregularly shaped white cap like little stalactites.

I am so confident of my mushroom-hunting skills that I initiate my culinary students into the secrets of *la cueillette* whenever nature permits. I remember one initiate in particular. He was fascinated, he said, by the stories his grandmother had told him of her childhood in Russia when she would go into the forests near her village and gather mushrooms to bring home to her mother to cook. Even though he traveled frequently to Russia, he had never been mushroom hunting and had selected my program specifically for the foraging component. He could hardly wait.

I took him and the other five in the group into the forest between Aups and Salernes late one afternoon the day they arrived. We had been visiting a winery and the forest was on the way home. It was a reasonably good mushroom season that year, but not great, and in the coming twilight he filled his basket with everything he could find, from rotting *pisacanes* to several very respectable *sanguins,* calling out with excitement over every find.

The next morning he got up early, skipped breakfast, and went directly to the forest on his own, returning with another basket of mushrooms for me to peruse. I covered the kitchen table with newspapers and we took out his finds, one by one, laying them on the paper. Again he had a big selection of *pisacanes* in poor condition and several decent *sanguins*, plus a pockmarked *Boletus satanas*, and a dozen or more other mushrooms, all *pas bon* to one degree or another.

"And what about this one?" he'd say, holding up an elegant lavender-gray specimen, or a meaty-looking, brownish red one. *"Pas bon,"* I'd have to say, and then watch his face fall as I pointed to the icon representing an empty plate in my mushroom guide, meaning that it wasn't poisonous, just not good to eat.

"But it looks good," he'd say.

"I know, some of them are so pretty and smell so good, it's hard to believe they aren't good to eat."

After taking photographs, he reluctantly let me discard all the *pas bons*, and then I taught him and the others how to clean the good ones, how to look for worms, and finally how to cook them. He had found, in his two sorties, about twelve edible mushrooms. We chopped them, then sautéed them with olive oil, garlic, salt, and pepper and put them on toasts to have with our *apéritif* at lunch that day, where he took more photographs of us all eating his wild mushrooms. The rest of the week, whenever he had a chance, he'd wander off into the forest, looking for mushrooms. He also bought as many different ones as he could find in the open markets.

People who come to my culinary program always ask me about truffles in the same breath they ask about mushrooms, which is understandable since they are all fungi, but there are meaningful differences between the two. First is the season. The frosts that kill the mushrooms are needed to ripen the famous black truffles, so the truffle season is in winter, not fall, and usually lasts until mid- to late February.

The most important difference is habitat. Truffles, which are tubers, grow underground in association with a host tree—oak, hazelnut, pine, or linden—and the spores of the tuber produce filaments that elongate and attach to the roots of the host tree. From this union, mycorrhizae are formed, and eventually the tree's root system is invaded. Only a trained dog or pig can sniff out truffles, or a very practiced eye might be able to see the tiny flies that lay their eggs in the ground above a truffle.

Within the last twenty years or so, truffle farming has grown significantly, because INRA, the Institut national de la recherche agronomique, developed the technology to successfully inoculate oak, hazelnut, and other seedling trees with the spores of *Tuber melanosporum*. The seedlings are planted in groves, just like olives, and are cultivated. After approximately eight years, the trees begin yielding an annual crop of black truffles. A higher percentage of truffle-bearing trees is produced using inoculated seedlings than by the traditional method of planting acorns gathered in the wild from truffle-bearing trees, a highly popular technique during the nineteenth century.

In the nineteenth century, Périgord became known for black truffles, which soon came to be called Périgord truffles. During the apogee of truffle production at the end of the nineteenth century, black truffles from Provence and elsewhere were sent to the brokers in Périgord, who then shipped the "Périgord truffles," now synonymous with luxury, to Paris and the capitals of the world. The name has stuck, even though 80 percent of the recorded truffle harvest today comes from Provence.

I didn't learn about truffles when Donald, Ethel, and I lived in Provence. Nor did I ever hear much about them when we spent our summer vacations there. It wasn't until Jim, my second husband, and I went to Provence one winter to do research for a book that I discovered a whole new culinary adventure awaited me.

My editor had told me I couldn't write about food in Provence without including truffles. However, I had almost no experience of them. I had never found one, only read about them, and the several times I had eaten them (they were preserved) I found them tasteless. My mission that winter was to find people to take me truffle hunting, to talk to people about truffles, and to eat as many fresh truffles as I could. I soon discovered that the truffle world is a secret, private one, far more so than the mushroom world.

Truffles are big business and can sell for upward of six hundred dollars a kilo, or around two pounds. Foragers hunt them on their own land or communal land, or lease private land for the truffle season, guard it against poachers, and keep, as much as possible, the amount of truffles they unearth and sell secret so they won't be taxed. Truffling is a clandestine affair, and I know of poachers who have been severely beaten when caught red-handed.

The object of their desire is the black truffle, *Tuber melanosporum*, called *rabasse* in Provençal. It looks like a lump of coal or a large dog's nose, dark and rough to the touch. It is roundish, irregular, and bumpy. It can be as small as the tip of your little finger, or as large as a grapefruit, but most of those I have seen since my initiation into the world of truffles lie somewhere in between. When freshly dug, still encased in mud and dirt, they could pass for darkish dirt clods. Cut open, a ripe truffle displays solid, dense flesh, veined gray and white. But more than the shape or color, it is the perfume that sets these fungi apart from all others: pungent, earthy, almost animal. Once I experienced this heady perfume during that first winter research trip, I became happily, gratefully, addicted.

100   It began with an old truffle hunter we were given an introduction to, M. Capretti. Jim and I went to visit him at his house. As we sat with him and his wife in their comfortable, well-appointed dining room, sipping coffee and eating *croquants*, the almond-flavored hard cookies that can be found in most *boulangeries*, he told us a story about how his grandfather took him truffle hunting as a young boy.

"My grandfather was too old to work in the vineyard and fields anymore. He took care of the *potager*, the vegetable garden, and me. My mother died when I was born. I went everywhere with my grandfather. He was a big man, even with his stooped shoulders. Bigger than most of the men around. Not like me." He laughed, because he was very small, barely taller than five feet.

"His nose was big, his hands were big, and his feet were big, but he was never clumsy. You couldn't even hear his step in the forest, it was so light."

"How old were you?" I asked.

"Oh, I must have been ten. Let's see, that would have been around 1925, after the war. My grandfather and father were both in it. Lucky to survive. Most of their friends from around here didn't. You can see their names engraved on the monument out there in the square. Laugier, Borne, Minarvois, Scaffone—I knew all their sons. They were my age. Not many of them left either now. Killed in the next war. We were with the partisans, the men from here. Most of us anyway."

His wife smiled proudly and got up from the polished wood table with its crocheted centerpiece and healthy African violet and went to the gleaming sideboard. She returned with a silver-framed photograph of half a dozen men standing with guns, their hats pulled low against the sun.

"We all slept in there." He pointed to the stone hut in the background. "Except whoever was on guard duty. Found some truffle trees in that forest, too. Never went back there, though."

After talking a little more about the war—I told him that my grandfather was killed in World War I and was buried in a Canadian military cemetery in France near Cambrai—the subject turned back to truffles.

"My grandfather showed me how to look for the *brûlés*, the circles around the base of the oak trees where all the grass is dead. Something happens when the truffles are growing that kills the grass. That first day we didn't take the *cochon*, the pig. He always hunted with a pig, just like I still do."

I let him continue.

"'Jo Jo'—that's what my grandfather called me—'I'm going to show you how to find truffles with no pig, no dog, no nothing. Just your wits. If you can find them, you can sell them. Then you will always have money. This is part of your inheritance, this knowledge, but you must work for it.'

"That day he showed me how to break off a branch of Aleppo pine—there're lots of those in our forests—then tear off all but the top needles to make a switch. We hovered over one of the *brûlés* and my grandfather gently brushed the ground with the tip of the switch. 'Ah, aha,' he said, 'look! There they are. See those flies? That means there're truffles here.'"

The truffle fly, *Suillia gigantea*, drawn like a magnet to the perfume of the truffles, lays its eggs in the truffled ground, providing a clue for the pigless, dogless hunter.

M. Capretti sat back and smiled. "Ah, those were happy days."

"How did you dig them up?"

"My grandfather had a tool he used, like a screwdriver. He pushed it gently into the ground until he hit the truffle. They're pretty hard. Then, he loosened the soil around it and pulled it out. It was a big one, too." He got up and went into the kitchen.

"Like this one." He held up a lumpy black truffle the size of a large grapefruit. I had never seen one that big in real life, only in photographs.

"May I hold it?"

He wagged his finger at me. "*Ah, non.* This one is already sold to a restaurant. I don't want anything to happen to it. Good price too. It weighs half a kilo, so that's twelve hundred francs." At that time that was more than two hundred dollars.

After returning the truffle to its hiding place, he said, "Truffles have been good to me. I've never had any other job or occupation, just truffles. In fact, when my father died and left me the farm and vineyard, I pulled out all the grapes and planted oak trees instead. I could always buy wine—I didn't need to make it—better to have truffles."

Our visit ended with a trip to one of his *truffières*, or truffle plantations. M. Capretti buttoned a hand-knit woolen vest on over his plaid shirt and pulled a brown felt hat over his curly gray hair, all of which made him look, with his rosy apple cheeks and bright little eyes, like a hobbit. We then walked a couple of doors down from his house to a stone garage. He turned a heavy key in the lock and swung the doors open to reveal, alongside a shiny white Renault van, a fenced pen holding a snorting pig.

"Just bought the Renault last year. Brand-new it is." He laughed, patting it.

"Truffles have been good to me." The van was parked with the rear door facing the pig's pen. He opened the door and propped a wooden ramp against the bed, which had a thick layer of fresh hay.

"Cou cou, cou cou, ma belle," M. Capretti chimed as we turned to the pig. "Yes, my girl, time to go out for treats. Yes, indeed." He slipped her something from his pocket as he opened the gate of her pen. He clucked as she pranced up the ramp on her pointed feet, following his hand, which held another treat.

Long and lean with rosy skin showing beneath white bristles, his pig reminded me of Lucretia, the sow that Donald and I had bought so many years before. I hadn't known about truffles then. I wondered if there had been truffles in the forest near our goat barn and if Lucretia would have been able to sniff them out.

In the old days, people used to take their pigs into the forest to feed on fallen acorns, and I was told that the talented pigs would find truffles and root them up. The hunter-gatherer needed to be close at hand, just as he does today, or the pig would eat the entire find.

M. Capretti, like other pig users, kept his pig on a leash. The leash is quickly jerked the minute the pig "marks," or scents, a truffle. At that moment the pig lunges forward, forty to a hundred kilos or more of muscle, depending upon the age of the pig, straining to get at the truffle, rip it out of the ground with its powerful snout, and eat it. The wily handler pops him a dog biscuit instead, turning the animal's head with one hand, while reaching into the ground to lift out the truffle with the other. M. Capretti slipped the prize so quickly and discreetly into his pouch that I couldn't see it, even though I was right next to him. Some hunters put a ring in the pig's nose to prevent it from digging, but M. Capretti said he felt that was cruel and showed laziness on the part of the owner.

"You need to be skillful. If you're skillful, no need to hurt the pig. She's your friend."

When I asked him if he ever used a dog instead of a pig, he shrugged his shoulders and said, "Oh, sometimes." In his opinion it was better to have the pig. That way, in a year or two, you'd have hams and *pâté* as well as truffles. However, pigs are rarely used for truffle hunting in Provence today, due, I suspect, to their size and the difficulty of moving them around, as well as the need to supply them food, lodging, and housekeeping all year.

Dogs are mostly preferred now, and the breed of dog is not important—almost any kind can be trained to find truffles. It is more about the dog's intelligence and relationship to its master than about breed. I've gone hunting with dachshunds, Bernese mountain dogs, springer spaniels, and mutts, and seen many more breeds performing at truffle trials, contests where hunters pit their dogs against one another to see whose dog can find the secret, buried truffles the fastest.

When I asked one old Provençal about how he trained his dogs, he shrugged. "*Ma foi.* It's easy. You give him a smell of truffle, let him know it, to get used to the smell. I put a truffle in a sock, tie it in, then toss it, let him go get it, and reward him with a biscuit. Then I hide the sock, all different places. When he brings back the sock all the time, I start burying the truffle so he knows to smell it under the earth. Then, in the *truffière* or in the forest, he will look for it. Of course, the dog has to have a good palate to begin with."

I'm not so sure about that, because the dogs, unlike the pigs, don't try to dig up the truffle once they've marked it. Instead, they sit there, waiting for their treat, more interested in being rewarded by their master for their good work than in eating the truffle.

On returning to M. Capretti's house, we started to say our good-byes, but he stopped us. "Wait a minute," he said, hurrying up his stairs. He came back with a glass canning jar with five eggs in it. He flipped the metal ring on the jar to open it, pulled a few truffles out of his pouch, and put them in the jar, fitting them among the eggs before refastening the ring.

"These are eggs from my chickens, good eggs. You keep them and the truffles together in the jar. The smell of the truffles goes into the eggs. In two days, even three, break the eggs into a bowl, clean the truffles, and grate them into the eggs. Let stand a little, add some sea salt, and then cook the eggs in butter to make your *oeufs brouillés*. Ahhh." He kissed the tip of his fingers with a smack. "Sublime. *Vous verrez.*"

We did as we were told, and whenever we're in Provence during truffle season, we make our traditional *brouillé*, eating it with thin toasts and a glass of local red wine, bathing in the powerful, sensual aroma of every bite. We grate truffles over mashed potatoes, sliver them over salads, slice them onto grilled bread, and drizzle olive oil over them, along with a sprinkling of sea salt. We try to attend one of the many community truffle feasts held during January and February, often put on by local chapters of the Confrérie de la Truffe du Mort Ventoux et du Combat Venaissin, an association of truffle lovers. At the feasts, we, like the hundreds of other people there, tuck into four, five, even six courses, all featuring truffles.

Poulet au genièvre farci aux champignons sauvages
JUNIPER-RUBBED CHICKEN STUFFED
WITH WILD MUSHROOMS

While walking through the forests of Provence looking for mush-rooms, I notice that the scent of juniper is almost as strong as the damp, fungal scent of the forest floor. I like to fill a pocket with the deep purple juniper berries and later use them to cook with mushrooms, re-creating the memory of the forest and the hunt.

Start by rubbing a frying chicken inside and out with two or three pinches of ground juniper berry mixed with some fine sea salt and freshly ground black pepper. (Juniper berries are easy to grind using a mortar and pestle or an electric grinder, and the fragrance released is reason enough to do it.) Preheat an oven to 350 degrees F.

Melt a nubbin of butter in a frying pan, and add a large spoonful or two of minced shallots, two generous handfuls of *chanterelles, cèpes*, hedge-hogs, or other wild mushrooms, the large ones sliced, the small ones cut in half or left whole. You can mix in brown and white button mushrooms if you are short on wild ones. Sauté the mushrooms and shallots, seasoning them with salt, pepper, and ground juniper. When the vegetables are barely golden, put them in a bowl with their juices, add cubes of day-old *baguette* or other sturdy rustic bread, and toss everything together. Add a pinch or two of fresh thyme leaves. Stuff the chicken cavity with the mixture and truss the legs with kitchen twine.

Put the chicken in a roasting pan and roast it, basting occasionally with the pan juices, until it is fragrant and golden brown and the juices run clear when an inner thigh is pierced with the tines of fork.

Remove the chicken to a cutting board and cover it lightly with foil. Pour off the fat in the roasting pan and place it over medium-high heat. Add two handfuls of mushrooms to the pan and sauté them until they are golden. Pour in 1 cup of dry white wine or dry vermouth and scrape up any clinging bits. Set aside while you carve the chicken and arrange it on a platter with the stuffing in the center. Reheat the pan juices and mushrooms, pour over the chicken and stuffing, and serve.

SERVES 4

CHAPTER 4

BOUILLABAISSE FOR ALL

*M. Bruno displays his catch. An authentic Marseillais recipe.
Tasting history. The brothers' fête.*

During the brief time we kept goats and made cheese, we were
welcomed by the people of the small community where we lived,
all of them eager to share their knowledge of the local food and
customs, no one more so than M. Bruno.

One spring day, when Oliver was only five months old, we
were at M. and Mme. Bruno's home where we had been invited
for an *apéritif.* He was holding forth on *bouillabaisse* as Donald
and I sampled his *vin de noix*, a fortified wine he had produced
by macerating green walnuts in red wine with sugar and *eau-de-
vie.* "You can't make *bouillabaisse* with just any fish," he said.

"Mon mari," beamed his wife, *"mon mari* makes the true
Marseille *bouillabaisse*, you know. He's a Marseillais. He grew
up there and that's where he lived before he joined the Legion."
She nodded, "Yes, I met him because he was in Indochine with
the French Foreign Legion. I lived in the country, just outside

Hanoi. My grandmother was one of the earliest colonists. Her husband had a big butcher shop, the biggest in Hanoi. She rode horseback all over with her servants." As Mme. Bruno became more and more animated, her hands fluttering, her eyebrows lifting, and her mouth alternately pursing and smiling, it became increasingly difficult for me to follow the thread of her story. Her husband never interrupted her, just smiled and nodded and let her continue until she paused for breath. It was a story I had heard before, and was to hear many times again. With each telling, more of their personal history was pieced together, though I never got quite all of it before he died and she moved away.

"Now, the *bouillabaisse*. Have you had it before?" We had once, in Marseille, but I had only a vague memory of bowls of fish, shellfish, and a garlicky sauce. I had a stronger memory of the candlelit table where the two of us had sat facing the boats of the Vieux Port one October night, a few weeks before Donald and I got married. We stayed up late and walked along the *quai* of the port until we could see the Château d'If, where Dumas's Count of Monte Cristo had been imprisoned.

"Ah, that's good. And good you had it in Marseille," M. Bruno said. "Other places have different versions, but in Marseille you can find the true *bouillabaisse*. But listen, why don't I make it for you? You like to cook, Georgeanne, and I, a true Marseillais, will show you exactly how to make it. Can you come next Sunday—is that a good day for you? Next Sunday? I will bring the fish from Marseille. You have to have certain ones, you know. Well?"

"Yes," we said in unison. Although the goats' milk was in full flow, we could have all our morning work done early. I didn't sell the cheese to any Sunday markets, and Donald had Sundays off from his chicken delivery job. It was a relatively free day for us, and I loved the idea of learning to cook something with M. Bruno, especially something as special as *bouillabaisse*.

"Good, good." He rubbed his hands together.

We were sitting outside on their small flagstone terrace, near the brick barbecue he had just finished building. Red tulips were blooming against the gray stone wall that ran along the gravel driveway down to their house from the upper road. We could see across the vineyards in the valley to the forest beyond and, if we stood on our tiptoes, the roofs of the barns at the edge of the forest where we kept our goats and pigs.

"So, next Sunday morning come here at 10:30. I'll show you the fish and explain each step to you. *La petite*, Ethel, can play with my collection of stones." Ethel loved looking at his stones, all of which he had found in and around the valley. Some had fossils embedded in them, others were actual fossils, like fragments of dinosaur bones. Others were remnants of Gallo-Roman pottery. "Jocelyne can look after the baby while we cook. Will that be all right?"

"Of course," I said. Jocelyne, Mme. Bruno to me, was very fond of Oliver, and when he was born had given him a traditional Provençal baby-carrying basket made of woven willow. She trimmed it in antique cotton lace, sewing through the upper edge of the willow, and had made bedding to match. The basket had two handholds threaded with wide bands of blue satin ribbon plus heavy white cord, for hanging in the olive trees, she explained, while the parents were working. Inside the basket was a quilted Provençal baby cape and cap. I still have the basket, but recently passed on the lace and the cape to Oliver and his wife for their baby.

As kind as Mme. Bruno was to us, her intensity made me anxious. M. Bruno had exactly the opposite effect on me. It was going to be fun to cook with him.

III

The next Sunday, which was very clear and bright, we arrived at the Brunos', bringing several of our fresh cheeses.

"Oh, thank you, thank you." M. Bruno said, unwrapping one and bringing it up to his nose, breathing deeply. "Ah, so sweet, so fresh. Bravo! You have done a wonderful job with your cheeses. *Ils sont les vrais fromages de chèvre d'autrefois*—the real goat's-milk cheeses of the past."

I felt my face flush. Although he and many others had told me this before, each time I heard my cheeses praised made me feel proud of what we had done. It was an especially important compliment coming from him because he loved and appreciated good food and wine and was knowledgeable about their origins. He knew how to make goat's- and sheep's-milk cheeses, to cure meats, to slaughter and butcher, to raise animals of all kinds, to choose the best fish and shellfish, and to make wine and *vin maison* and liqueurs. He also knew where to find wild asparagus and mushrooms. He was, like so many Provençal men I've met since, fascinated by local ingredients and food and how to cook them, and far more interested in talking about that than about his work. I never heard about what occupation M. Bruno pursued, other than his wife's references to his years in the Legion, and some apartment properties that were occasionally mentioned as a reason for needing to return to Marseille where they lived most of the year.

"Let's put these cheeses on a platter—I brought a couple of sheep's-milk cheeses from Marseille for you to try, plus some of the *Brousse* I told you about, the one that is made in le Rove, not far from my cousin's house—and then we'll start our *bouillabaisse*."

Their house was not a farmhouse or a *bastide*, or a villa or a manor house, the four most common country places in the area. Farmhouses, or *mas*, range from large rambling affairs to small compact ones. *Bastides* are large farmhouses that could also serve as a fortification. *Villa* is the term used to describe large, rather important freestanding houses with garden or land, often recently built on the edges of villages as well as in the country. Rural manor houses are large, multistoried, and square or rect- angular, and the approach to them is often lined with long alleys of plane or poplar trees. 113

The Brunos' residence was a small two-story stone house with a red tile roof, set just below a narrow dirt road on a rise of land cut out from the *garrigue*-covered hillside, thick with scrub oak and juniper. Its plastered walls were painted pale chalk blue, a color popular in the 1930s, with wooden shutters stained dark brown and decorative iron grating on the lower windows and the window of the front door. It had no barns or lofts, just a recently built garage, so it was not a farmhouse. It was too small and mod- est to be a proper villa, and it was certainly not a manor house. I have never seen a house quite like it.

The front door opened directly into a square foyer with a massive, carved wooden staircase, more appropriate for a *château* than their small house, that twisted up to the second floor. The foyer was crowded with several small gilded tables whose spindly legs supported ebony statuary, carved boxes, pieces of jade and rose quartz, and a few large fossils. One table held a lamp with a maroon silk shade fringed in gold. Just behind the door was an elephant-leg umbrella stand, and, off to the side, a coat rack and a decorative cabinet. There was just room to move through the foyer to the stairs or to turn either right toward the bathroom door or left into the living room. The space felt a little claustro- phobic, as did the rest of the house.

A round dining table, lit by a green glass chandelier, was in the corner of the living/dining room, which also held a large maroon tufted sofa, two overstuffed leather chairs, an Oriental rug on the tile floor, a curio cabinet in one corner topped with a record player, and a built-in armoire in another corner. The walls were devoted to bookshelves, oil and watercolor still lifes (M. Bruno's own work—and quite good), and a large clock. In the back of the living room was a doorway opening to the right, into the kitchen.

"This way, this way." M. Bruno led the way through the living room maze to the kitchen doorway.

"It's all in here. I picked it up this morning at the quai des Belges. The boats come in every morning there to unload their catch from the previous night. It's a wonderful place. The fish-mongers are, well, they can be pretty coarse, but, that's part of it. The important thing is the fish."

"Now, first of all," continued our guide, "I must tell you that it is very odd to be making *bouillabaisse* for only six of us." I thought it was nice that he included Ethel in the table count. The French think children are never too young to learn how to eat. "The minimum, the *minimum*, would normally be eight, but best of all, ten, twenty, forty—the more the better, because one of the secrets of a great *bouillabaisse* is the number and variety of the fish that are used."

He rolled up his sleeves and tied on a white apron, covering his hand-knit brown sweater-vest and ample midsection. He was about fifty at the time, and his brown hair had begun to thin and recede, showing more olive skin. His brown eyes twinkled as he talked, and whenever he smiled a dimple appeared to the right of his chin. For a Marseillais, known for the volubility of their arms and hands, his were, unlike his wife's, restrained. I wondered if it was the influence of his time spent in Asia, where he had said he'd practiced Buddhism.

"Look. Here are the fish." He opened the metal cooler at his feet and I saw a dozen or more whole fish laid on ice, plus a perforated metal container and some wet burlap bags. He tapped the container. "These are the *favouilles,* the little crabs. I have to keep them separate from the fish or they'll gnaw on them."

The kitchen was tiny, with one small window above the composite granite sink, a waist-high refrigerator next to it, a stove against the rear wall, and a pantry. Pots and pans hung overhead. A curtain of traditional red Provençal fabric in tiny print gathered on a wire covered the open space and shelves beneath the sink and the countertop. I could have stretched out my arms in the middle of the kitchen and touched both hands, palms flat, to the opposing walls.

We stood hip to hip, as M. Bruno laid one fish after another onto a large, fennel-covered platter, discoursing on the culinary attributes and habitats of each fish while showing me the key signs of quality and freshness to look for. I was fascinated.

"Now this is St-Pierre, and it comes from the deep waters." He laid out a silver flatfish that seemed to be half head, its back crowned with sprays of spiny fins. I found it beautiful and wondered what it had looked like only hours ago, cutting silently through the sea.

"You can always tell St-Pierre by the dark spot behind the eyes. This is a white fish, one of the tender ones we'll add toward the end of the cooking." I could clearly see the dark, round spot, almost a smudge, nearly in the middle of the fish.

Before I could ask why it was called St-Pierre, he told me. "It got its name because Saint Pierre, the apostle fisherman, was said to have left his mark when he grasped the fish, pressing his thumb there while he looked in his pockets for money to pay tribute to the Romans." I reached out and pressed my thumb into the smudge, remembering my Sunday school lessons about the big fisherman.

Several brownish red fish with bulging heads and fins as sharp as pins followed. They looked familiar to me, like the small, mottled fish my brother and I used to catch off the rocks in Southern California. We called them sculpin, or scorpionfish, and we were told to throw them back because they weren't good to eat, being bony and tasting of iodine. "These, the *rascasse*," M. Bruno said, pointing to the small fish, "are essential to *bouillabaisse*. And they must be cooked whole, with their heads. Bony these rockfish are, but with a fine flavor and firm flesh. You'll see." I wondered if we could have cooked our sculpin after all—and whether not eating them was dictated by custom rather than by taste.

Next came another rockfish, the *galinette*, followed by a small eel, so flexible it seemed still alive, and then a largish, silver-black fish. "Now look at this. Isn't it splendid?" He slid it from his hands onto the laden platter.

"Look how clear and bright the eyes are, the skin so slippery—all the signs of a *poisson du jour*, no more than twenty-four hours out of the sea. Of course, everything I have today I bought this morning off a boat. But, this, the *loup de mer*, is my favorite fish, with its tender flesh, sweet and full of the taste of the depths of the sea."

One of the burlap bags revealed a large hunk of monkfish. "A very ugly fish, but good, firm flesh. This fish is an important element in a well-balanced *bouillabaisse*. And its head—there, look at that! Have you ever seen such a head?" he said as he turned another bag upside down, releasing a diamond-shaped, heavy-boned fish head, surely the pit bull of the fish world, its serpentine spine curling as it spun into the corner of the cooler, coming to rest in a ghoulish coil. I had never seen a monkfish, but I certainly agreed that it was ugly. More fish heads tumbled out of another bag.

"Before we begin the *fond*, though, we need to season our fish. Here. Sprinkle this over them all. Be generous." The *fond*, I had learned, was the base of the soup. He handed me a wine bottle fitted with a stainless-steel spout. I had seen these before, so I knew it was olive oil, bought in bulk then bottled at home, just like wine, something Donald and I were starting to do. I doused the fish while M. Bruno sprinkled them with sea salt, pepper, and saffron threads.

"And now, some fennel seeds." He rubbed a head of dried wild fennel between his fingers and the seeds scattered across the surface of the fish. I picked up some and did the same, releasing the sharp, sweet scent of licorice. He laid more fronds of fresh, bright green fennel, abundant now in late spring, across the fish. My nose tickled, there was so much fennel in the kitchen.

We spent another half an hour making the *fond* for the *bouillabaisse*. Ethel and Donald came in and out of the kitchen as we cooked. Ethel, intrigued especially by the fish on the platter, checked the fins and sharp teeth of the *rascasse*, comparing them to the delicately etched mouth of the *loup de mer*. "These are much prettier, don't you think, Mom? That one," she said, poking the side of the *rascasse*, "looks scary and sharp." I thought again of pulling sculpin from the seaweed beds off the rocks, taking them off the hooks, and throwing them back, carefully holding each one in a towel so I wouldn't get stabbed by the fins.

The *fond* began with olive oil, and we added leeks, onion, garlic, and tomatoes, along with freshly gathered wild thyme, sautéing everything in a large kettle until the kitchen was filled the fragrance of the earth. Then the fish heads and bones from the cooler went into the pot, along with the small crabs and the eel from the platter. I watched as the meat changed from opalescent to opaque, and the skulls began to emerge as the meat softened and fell away from the bones.

"Keep stirring while I get the *petits poissons*." Reaching into the cooler, M. Bruno pulled out a bag, opened it, and gently poured a rainbow of two or three dozen small fish, some no larger than my little finger, into the pot of hot oil and vegetables. Their red, orange-yellow, and olive-green hues quickly turned a uniform gray, their bright eyes sinking and becoming white with the heat.

"These little rockfish give the *fond* its richness. Like the *rascasse*, the *petits poissons* are essential." As he stirred, the fish gradually broke down and melted into the vegetables. Water and a length of dried orange peel were added, along with salt and pepper. As the stock simmered, the aroma subtly changed from the scent of the hills to that of the sea.

While the soup base simmered, M. Bruno led me through the steps of making the *rouille*, the garlicky, red pepper–based mayonnaise that we were to eat with the soup. We sliced a *baguette* and put the slices in the oven to dry (never grill them, he said), and then rubbed the rough dry bread with garlic cloves.

Donald and Ethel had gone for a walk, looking for old Roman tiles. I stepped outside onto the terrace to visit Oliver, who was cooing and kicking his feet and waving his little arms in his baby chair while Mme. Bruno set the table under the chestnut tree, talking to him all the time. I walked to the edge of the terrace and looked out across the silent valley to the beginning of the Alps in the distance and thought how lucky I was to be experiencing this life. Then, after kissing Oliver, I went back into the kitchen.

The *fond* was finished, and we put it into an large, old-fashioned food mill, turning the handle until the crabs, fish heads, *petits poissons*, eel, herbs, vegetables, and liquid were transformed into a thick, brownish gold soup. The fish bones and other debris were left behind in the mill and discarded. We strained the soup through a large, cone-shaped *chinois*, just to make sure there were no bones. As I held the *chinois* while M. Bruno poured, I was enveloped with the fragrance of the soup. I was getting hungry and my mouth was watering in anticipation.

When we finished straining, we put the soup into a large, clean pot. My teacher set the flame to simmer before pouring *pastis* for everyone. Donald and Ethel had returned by then with a bag full of finds, which M. Bruno exclaimed over and promised to peruse in detail after lunch. He passed around a plate of toasts with *pâté* and I ate several while he continued to talk about *bouillabaisse*.

"The secret, the truth of the *bouillabaisse*, is in the boiling. The olive oil makes a *liaison* with the broth, and the fish are roughly handled by the boil, giving them a raggedy look. If the fish are not a little ragged, the *bouillabaisse* was not made correctly." He smiled and wagged his finger at me. "Remember that the next time you have it at a restaurant."

As we sipped our *pastis*, M. Bruno added a cup of soup with dissolved saffron threads, stirring it into the soup, then slid in the firm-fleshed fish, which must be cooked first, checking his watch. The soup, now on high heat, boiled over the top of the fish, and I watched in fascination as their skin broke slightly and whole chunks began to flake as they went from raw to cooked. When exactly twelve minutes had passed, he added the more delicate St-Pierre and the red mullets. These he cooked for six minutes.

"Ah," he smiled, "smell that." He was leaning over the pot, fanning the rising steam toward his nostrils. "There is nothing like a good *bouillabaisse*. Nothing." Donald and I copied him, sweeping our hands over the soup to bring us the aroma of the sea made fragrant with saffron and orange. Ethel insisted on being lifted up so she too could wave her hand over the steaming soup, sampling it on the air.

M. Bruno gently removed the whole fish and chunks of monkfish to a platter. He ladled the soup into a tureen and set both on the table, which was already holding baskets of warm bread and bowls of *rouille*. M. Bruno instructed us to put a piece of bread into each of our shallow, rimmed soup plates and then ladled some of the soup over it. We helped ourselves to the spicy *rouille* that he passed, spooning it onto the softening bread. M. Bruno told us to eat while he filleted the fish, but first he filled our wineglasses with *vin blanc de Cassis,* the crisp white wine that comes from just east of Marseille.

What a taste! The bread rapidly became soft enough to cut off bites with a spoon, which I dredged in the *rouille* and the thick, intensely flavored soup. The explosion of flavors and textures was unforgettable. With each spoonful, the combination became better, and I kept thinking, how is it possible that this elixir was made with fish heads and bones, small crabs, and fish almost too small to identify? Soon my bowl was empty, and as I looked around, I saw the other bowls were empty as well. It was time for the fish.

When our host finished his tableside display of the deftest boning I have ever seen, he offered us the fish, serving us some of each, then ladling more soup into our bowls, again passing the *rouille* and bread. Each fish had its distinct taste and texture, contributing to the wonder of the *bouillabaisse.*

"*Très, très bon, chéri,*" exclaimed Mme. Bruno. "The fish are perfectly cooked, just the way your father would have done it. Bravo!" We chimed in with our compliments as well. Even though we had nothing to compare it to, we were sure we were eating the true Marseille *bouillabaisse*.

....

The quai de Belges, bordering Marseille's Vieux Port, is still the place to buy the freshest fish and shellfish right off the fishing boats. Many that pull up to the quai are registered in Marseille, indicated by the letters "MA," for Marseille, following the registration numbers lettered on the sides of the boats. A lot of them are owned by families that have been fishing for generations. Knowledge of the secret places where the rocky shorelines shelter the *rascasse* and eels, the exact locations and fathoms for St-Pierre and *dorade*, and which stretches of sandy open spaces along the bottom hold the flatfish, has been passed down from father to son.

Marseille has been an important port ever since it was founded in the sixth century B.C.E. It is at the crossroads of Europe, Asia, and Africa, and through it at one time flowed all the foodstuffs and goods of the known world. Pilgrims set sail from here to the Holy Land and immigrants arrived here from France's once-extensive colonies. The flavor and taste of the city's exotic history come together in *bouillabaisse*, its most famous dish.

Like all traditional dishes, *bouillabaisse* is saturated with lore and history. Every family, every port, and every neighborhood along the coast between Marseille and Toulon prepares a version. There is even a Marseillais legend that says Venus fed it to her husband, Vulcan, so that, once satiated, he would sleep while she carried on a dalliance with Mars. According to some stories, the soup was brought to Marseille by Greek mariners from Phocaea, in Asia Minor, who founded the city. These fishermen, and those who followed over the centuries, were purported to have boiled the leftover, unsalable, even spoiled bits of their catch in sea-water. Scholars have found no mention in historical documents that would substantiate this tale. Some say that because the water of the Mediterranean is so salty, such a soup would be unpalatable, if not inedible.

The name *bouillabaisse* is thought to have originated from *bouillir*, to boil, and *abaisser*, to turn down. *Abaisser* also means, in culinary usage, to reduce, which makes sense in this context because as the soup boils it reduces. Although the primary meaning of *abaisser* is to lower, the heat must be kept on high not only to reduce the contents but to create the essential *liaison* of olive oil and broth that, along with impeccably fresh fish and saffron, defines a good *bouillabaisse*.

Travelers in the 1800s, including Mark Twain, Émile Zola, and Gustave Flaubert, mentioned *bouillabaisse* when describing their sojourns in Marseille, as did the famous French gastronome Curnonsky, who called it *soupe d'ôr*, golden soup, and raved about its essence and flavors.

By the mid-1800s, Marseille and the Côte d'Azur had been discovered by the rich, and fancy hotels and restaurants vied with one another for fame and for the customers who were passing through their city. During this period, the golden soup as it is now classically made emerged, flavored not only with olive oil and garlic, but also with saffron, fennel, orange peel, onion, tomatoes, and aromatics.

The *bouillabaisse* with which most of us are familiar—a clear, sparkling broth laced with chunks of white fish, shrimp, mussels, and even scallops and lobster—has little in common with the *bouillabaisse* one finds in the best of the coastal restaurants from Nice to Marseille. A Charte de la bouillabaisse, created in 1980 and signed by eleven restaurants, most of them in Marseille, states the ingredients and the method of preparing and serving a "true" *bouillabaisse*. This came about because an increasing number of dishes being served as *bouillabaisse* strayed far from the original version, endangering the very nature of the soup. The charter allows more flexibility than M. Bruno would have permitted. It acknowledges that shellfish can be added, as can potatoes, and that *aïoli* can be served as well as *rouille*. For the rest of the ingredients and the style of service, M. Bruno's version would have fit exactly the parameters for a true *bouillabaisse* according to the charter.

123

....

Long after Ethel and Oliver were grown, and I was teaching cooking classes in Provence, two brothers, both commercial fishermen, bought the big farmhouse at the bottom of my road and divided it into two adjoining living quarters. It had belonged to one of their uncles, their mother's brother, and they had often been visitors to the house, so they were familiar with most of the villagers and their extended families and friends.

Once a year in the fall they put on a semiprivate *bouillabaisse* feast, inviting eighty to a hundred people, charging everyone approximately twenty euros, just enough to cover their costs. The event includes *apéritifs*; *hors d'oeuvres*; *bouillabaisse* served correctly, according to the charter, in two courses; and a dessert. I discovered the event when a friend invited me to make up her party of six. I had just finished four week-long sessions of classes, and I looked forward to doing something different. The weather was still warm, as it so often is in late September, but the evenings could be chilly, so I brought along a wool shawl to wear over my long black linen sundress, because I knew we'd be eating outside until late.

I arrived just before 7:30, not wanting to be too early, just in case no one I knew was there yet. The road on either side of the brothers' house was already jammed with cars, and one of their wheat fields, now free of crop, had been turned into a parking lot for the night, but I still had trouble finding a place for my car. Floodlights mounted on the edge of the farmhouse roof illuminated the scene below, where rows of tables dressed in white butcher's paper were laid out. Old-time farmers and full-time residents mingled with the European and French urbanites who had bought second homes in the area. Everyone was wearing versions of summer finery and milling around the *apéritif* table where two of the most handsome men in the village, both masons with prematurely gray hair, dark brown eyes, weathered skin, and muscled forearms, were pouring a choice of *pastis, rosé,* or Coca-Cola. Voices rose and fell on the air, cicadas clicked in the background, and the scent of garlic cooking in olive oil came from the depths of the garage under the house.

I immediately saw my friend Yvonne, waving me to her table. She leapt up and kissed me on both cheeks, then introduced me to her friends who were visiting from Germany. Everyone brings their own tableware to these affairs, and Yvonne's was Rosenthal white china—huge soup bowls that were mostly rim, the kind you see in Michelin-starred restaurants—flatware acquired on a recent trip to Thailand, crystal wineglasses, and heavy dark-orange linen napkins. Down the table I could see a wide variety of tableware glittering in the light. By contrast, the *apéritifs* were in plastic glasses, and the *hors d'oeuvres,* which were peanuts, potato chips, and bite-size squares of *pissaladière,* caramelized onion flat bread, had been handed out on small paper napkins.

"Come on, let's go see them cook." Yvonne grabbed my hand. She was a successful stage actress in Germany and also an excellent cook, voraciously interested in all things culinary. We headed straight to the garage, which a hundred years ago had probably housed carriages, but now held two huge woklike pans, each more than a meter in diameter and steaming with a broth whose fragrance of hills and sea reminded me instantly of M. Bruno's little kitchen. The pots were set on large gas rings built into a cement-block base about hip height. The rims of the pots rose almost to my waist, making them a good level for tending. The garage was deep and dark in the corners, but on the closer walls I could see hanging the leftover trappings of rural life: padded leather donkey collars, sieves for separating the grain from the chaff, and pitchforks and rakes of worked-smooth wood. Had we been in a restaurant they would have seemed kitschy attempts at authentic decor, but here, on an old family farm, they were a natural part of the setting, just like the rototiller and disc whose outlines I could see in the far corner.

Along one wall, under the pitchforks and rakes, were a dozen or more plastic bins filled with fish. The incandescent lights of the barn selectively reflected their bright eyes and glittering scales, creating an unlikely seascape deep in the barn. I could identify some of the fish. Small, bright orange mullets, considered a delicacy. St-Pierre, easy to identify because of the thumbprint. Fat chunks of monkfish, whose ugly heads I supposed had already gone into the soup base. A whole bin of the spiky, essential *rascasse,* and many more fish, black, greenish, bluish, and red, whose names I didn't know. More bins, filled with peeled potatoes, stood next to the fish. On a small table between two of the steaming pans was a ceramic canister of sea salt, a glass jar half full of saffron threads, a big basket of bay leaves and wild thyme, and two glasses of *pastis.* I stood a moment, inhaling the scent of the place, before Yvonne dragged me over to be introduced as the American who lived up the road.

The brothers, each armed with a long metal spoon, were tending the pots of simmering soup. We all agreed we had seen one another in passing and were happy to meet finally. Both wore short-sleeved cotton shirts and jeans. One was wearing a baseball cap backward. The other had brushed his thinning brown hair back from his forehead. Their faces were rosy from the steam and heat of the soup, and glistened with a faint sheen of sweat. I asked how much fish was in the bins.

"Oh, forty or fifty kilos are left. We brought up more than a hundred kilos, including the *favouilles*, but a lot went into the *fond* here," he said, as he stirred.

"Did you catch them all?" I asked, watching the golden soup as it rhythmically bubbled up, collapsed back, and rose again. I could just see the propane flames beneath the black bottom of the pots and feel their hissing warmth. The crowd outside had stopped milling, and people were beginning to sit down.

"Oh, not all. Most of them. We made a few trades. We had more of the deepwater fish, like the St-Pierre, fewer of the shallow-water rockfish, so we traded with another fisherman. We're all pretty friendly."

A lighted doorway suddenly shone in the dark rear of the garage, framing a woman carrying a basin. She came toward us.

"Eh, Jean, the *rouille* is ready. Just needs a little more soup." She indicated the ladle on the wooden table with a nod of her head and held out the basin. The closest brother scooped up some soup, poured it into the basin, and then stirred it until the stiff peaks of the reddish gold *rouille* softened and smoothed.

"*Bonsoir,*" she said smiling at me and Yvonne. "*C'est bon, n'est-ce pas?*"

We agreed that it was good, everything—the evening, the setting, the fish—all the time eyeing the basin of fragrant *rouille*, thinking that soon we would be slathering it on top of our dried bread, into the soup, on top of the fish.

"Go on, have a seat. We're ready to bring out the *rouille* and serve the soup."

We left the garage and hurried back to our seats just in time to get a piece of bread into our bowls before a woman approached our table, laughing and joking as she came down the row, spooning the thick *rouille* on top of the waiting bread. Someone else followed with soup.

Yvonne poured the red Vacqueyras wine she had brought from her cellar. I thought it was a little powerful for the soup, but she likes big red wines, and it tasted good as the evening began to chill. As we set upon the soup and the wine, voices rose with laughter and camaraderie, and I could feel a bond growing among us, created by the sheer joy of eating *bouillabaisse*, a dish that everyone, including me, had memories of.

My bread softened with the soup, the *rouille* melted into it, and with each bite I tasted the garlic, roasted red peppers, fennel, saffron, fish, crabs, and eel, no longer discrete but melding to form the taste and texture of the *fond*. We served ourselves more toast and took more *rouille* from the small bowls brought to the table, while women passed behind us with pots of steaming soup, ladling more into our bowls if we asked. I had two servings, plus extra toast, and then the fish began to arrive.

The deep platters were heaped with chunks of monkfish and fillets of red mullet and sea bass, plus buttery potatoes, tinted gold by the soup's saffron. I remembered that M. Bruno didn't put potatoes in his *bouillabaisse*, but had explained that the Toulonnais swear by the necessity of potatoes.

I found myself caught off-guard by the memories that the *bouillabaisse* evoked of my past life, when the children were little and life seemed simpler. I excused myself early, explaining to Yvonne that I was more tired than I had thought. I managed to extricate my car from the crowded field where I had parked and drove up the road into the night.

128

....

Not all *bouillabaisse* is made with the precise collection of fish that M. Bruno taught me and that my fishermen neighbors support. Nor are there vast numbers of adherents to the Marseille *bouillabaisse* charter, although it appears to be a worthy endeavor. Among the many Provençal recipes for other versions, one is made with sardines and another, the so-called one-eyed *bouillabaisse*, with a fried-egg topping. There is even a *bouillabaisse* made only with vegetables, and another with spinach. The key element is always the boiling, the *bouillir*, and the reduction, the *abaisser*, which creates the luscious *liaison* of broth and olive oil.

I am not among those who assert that true *bouillabaisse* can be made only with Mediterranean fish, as some purists do. One such purist is a Provençal chef and cookbook author who carried on at length about authentic *bouillabaisse* over a dinner he was serving at his recently opened *auberge* in the hills not far from Aups. He insisted on using the exact Mediterranean fish and on cooking the soup in an old seasoned pot, the kind that you have to go the flea markets or *brocantes* to purchase unless you inherited one from your great-grandmother. He went on to say that he couldn't abide cookbook writers who purported to write traditional Provençal recipes while including nontraditional ingredients or methods, just so the books would sell to the foreigners that swarm to Provence.

I felt a little put off by this, especially the part about the flea market pot, but I kept smiling and said nothing.

"These so-called writers, a lot of them not even Provençal, are writing shortcuts and wrong instructions about everything. They're writing for foreigners, just to sell the books." I wondered briefly if I should take this personally, and decided not to.

He continued, arms waving, telling us how, at a restaurant he once had near Ubraye, two hundred kilometers from the Mediterranean, he hired people to go to the quai des Belges in Marseille to buy the proper fish for him, then engaged taxi drivers to bring the fish to him in the mountains, at great expense, so important was it to have fresh, perfect fish for any dish, but most certainly for *bouillabaisse*.

"Now, it is almost time for the fish soup I've made tonight, which I am serving with a special sauce, a lot like *aïoli*, but not an *aïoli*." We were a small group of ten friends seated at one of the three tables in the dining room. The soup arrived, the individual bowls delivered to us by the chef's wife. He appeared next, with several bowls of sauce and placed them at intervals along the table.

"Spoon a little of the sauce into your soup bowls, just a little to start. It can be powerful, and it might not suit all your tastes." Among us, only Anne was French, the rest being German, Dutch, American, and Belgian, and all except me were year-round inhabitants of the region.

I was sitting next to Anne, who sniffed at the sauce and added two large soupspoons of the pale yellow, very thin sauce to her bowl.

Joanne, across from me, added some to her bowl, then took a spoonful of soup. "What can you tell us about the sauce? What is in it?"

The chef's wife started to answer, but he interrupted. "Olive oil, of course, garlic, salt, pepper, a little like *aïoli*, but not."

Joanne persisted. "Does it have eggs in it, then, like *aïoli*?"

He continued extolling the virtues of his sauce, until finally his wife, said, yes, there are eggs.

It was a very good soup, with big chunks of fish in a light broth of late-harvest tomatoes, *fumet*, saffron, and fennel, and it tasted warming on the late fall night that we were there. On the way home in the car, Joanne said, "I think his special sauce was nothing more than an *aïoli* that had broken."

I suspected she was right, but I also suspected that he would have not been happy to know that I was one of those traitorous cookbook writers he was excoriating, and to learn that my treason went so far as to believe that *bouillabaisse* can be made without having the exact fish from the Mediterranean, to say nothing of the ideal flea-market cauldron. I like to think M. Bruno and my fishermen neighbors would agree with me: If one adheres to the spirit of the soup, making the *fond*; selecting both firm-fleshed and delicate fish; boiling the broth and olive oil together; seasoning well with saffron, fennel, and orange peel; and serving in two courses—first the broth, toasts, and *rouille*, and then the fish, filleted tableside—everyone will agree that they are tasting paradise in a bowl.

My making *bouillabaisse* in California, with fish available at local fish markets, has resulted over and over again in happy memories for everyone, from standing together with me over the simmering pot of fish heads and bones, local crabs, and wild fennel gathered from the roadside, to the final moment of serving the boned fillets and correctly ragged chunks of fish. I made it for a small party celebrating Ethel and Laurent's wedding anniversary. I set my soup pot outside in the shade of the walnut tree over a propane burner and we all cooked together, step by step, just as M. Bruno had taught me, while Jim made sure that the toasts dried out in the oven and were well rubbed with garlic.

By the time we sat down at our long table set with linens I had bought in Provence, our glasses filled with chilled *rosé* from Bandol, the baskets of bread and bowl of *rouille* before us, we could almost smell the salt air of the Mediterranean, even though the fish were from the Pacific.

Bouillabaisse toulonnaise

BOUILLABAISSE, TOULON STYLE

Toulon-style *bouillabaisse* differs from the Marseille style in its inclusion of saffron-infused potatoes, which I happen to love, and sometimes mussels. Otherwise, the two styles are almost identical. A rich *fond*, or base, made from small fish and fish bones, aromatics, and tomatoes, is sieved, puréed, and brought to a rolling boil to cook various kinds of fish. The dish is served in two courses, the broth first, with garlic-rubbed, dried bread and *rouille*, a sauce made with garlic and red peppers. Next comes the fish, in chunks and fillets, served Toulon style with the golden potatoes. According to strict tradition, certain Mediterranean fish are required for *bouillabaisse*, but an excellent meal can be made with Pacific or Atlantic fish or a combination, as long as they are very fresh and not oily.

Buy about 4 pounds of small fish such as assorted rockfish and scorpionfish, small eels, fish heads, and backbones. The fish should not be oily types like sardines, salmon, or mackerel. Add a few blue or other small crabs the size of your hand. Also buy five or six chunks of monkfish and one or two other firm, white fish, plus several whole fish such as flounder, red mullet, and sea bass. Finally, buy 2 pounds or so of mussels, if you want to add these as well.

Lay the monkfish and whole fish on a platter and drizzle them with extra-virgin olive oil. Sprinkle with coarse sea salt, freshly ground black pepper, and fennel seeds, rubbing the seeds between your fingers to release their essence. If you have some fresh fennel stalks and fronds, add them, too. Sometimes people add a drizzle of *pastis* as well.

To make the *fond*, cover the bottom of a large, heavy-bottomed pot with a film of extra-virgin olive oil and heat it over medium heat. When it's hot, add a chopped leek or two, using only the white part, along with a chopped onion, a goodly amount of chopped garlic, and several tomatoes. It's best to peel the tomatoes first, so that when the *fond* is pressed through a sieve, the skins won't block the holes. Cook the vegetables, stirring, until they are very soft, about 10 minutes. Add the eels, heads, and bones, and continue to stir until the meat starts dropping away, another 5 to 10 minutes. Add the small fish and crabs, and continue to stir until they start to dissolve, another 5 to 10 minutes. Now add about 3 quarts water, 2 to 3 cups dry white wine such as a *blanc de Cassis,* a piece of dried orange peel, and several large pinches of coarse sea salt, some ground pepper, and several sprigs of fresh thyme tied together with several sprigs of fresh parsley and a bay leaf. Also add a stalk of fresh fennel, cut into short lengths. If you don't have a fennel stalk, coarsely chop a fennel bulb and add a dash of *pastis* to the soup. Increase the heat to high and bring to a boil, then reduce to low and let the *fond* simmer until the meat has fallen away from the bones, about 15 minutes.

While the *fond* is cooking, make the *rouille* by crushing a dried cayenne chile, seeds removed and discarded, in a mortar with a pestle. Add three or four cloves of garlic and a pinch of coarse sea salt and grind to a paste. Dissolve a pinch of saffron threads in a teaspoon of hot water, add to the mortar, and blend again into a paste. If your mortar is large enough, continue making the *rouille* in it, using the pestle. If not, scrape the mixture into a bowl. Whisk in an egg yolk until it is fully blended. Drop by drop, add extra-virgin olive oil, whisking continuously. As the mixture thickens, the oil can be added in a slow, steady stream. Continue to whisk

CONTINUED...

133

until the mixture is thickened and stiff, like mayonnaise. Set aside. Put slices of *baguette* on baking sheets and bake in a 300 degree F oven until they are dried but not browned, about 20 minutes. Remove them and rub both sides with garlic cloves.

When the *fond* is ready, remove it in batches to a fine-mesh sieve placed over a large bowl. Remove the stalks of fennel and the packet of herbs and discard them. Crush the contents, using a wooden spoon to extract all the juices, crushing until only the fish and vegetable debris remains. A food mill is excellent for this process if you have one. Discard the debris and repeat until all the *fond* has been crushed. Wash the sieve thoroughly. To be sure to catch any small bones, strain the *fond* again, this time into a clean soup pot. The *fond* can be prepared up to 12 hours in advance.

When you are ready to cook the fish, heat the *fond* to boiling and add two or three pinches of saffron dissolved in a little boiling water. Add five or six potatoes that have been peeled and quartered. Cook them for 5 minutes, then add the chunks of firm fish, any large whole fish, the mussels, and finally any fillets. Boil steadily, uncovered, for 10 to 15 minutes. The fish will become raggedy. The key to doneness is the tenderness of the potatoes. When they can be pierced easily with the tines of fork, remove the pot from the heat and gently lift out first the fillets, then the whole fish, chunks, and potatoes, placing them on a platter. Cover the platter loosely with foil. Add a spoonful or two of the broth to the *rouille* to smooth it out.

To serve, bring the garlic-rubbed bread and *rouille* to the table, instructing your guests to put a piece of bread in their soup bowls and top it will a dollop of *rouille*. Bring the *fond* to the table and ladle some into each bowl. After everyone has enjoyed the first course, bring out the platter of fish and potatoes. You can fillet the whole fish at the table or in the kitchen before serving it. Give everyone a piece or two of potato and a bit of each kind of fish, placing them in the bowls. Drizzle each serving with a bit of *fond* and pass the *rouille*.

SERVES 6 TO 10

LONG SUMMER MEALS

The fish man brings sardines. Cooking from Marcel and Marie's potager. Quinson lake. First dinner at Le Relais Notre-Dame. Bastille Day soup.

··············

For the first time in more than three years, Donald and I returned to Provence, able at last to take advantage of the long summer holiday afforded us now that we were teachers in California. Our first stop was Denys and Georgette Fine's, whose small rental we had lived in when Oliver was born. They were expecting us for lunch and before we could get out of the car, they ran out to greet us with hugs and kisses. Ethel remembered them and threw her arms around Georgette, but Oliver, who was a baby when we left, hung back, clasping his green Hulk doll. He had no memory of these people who were speaking a strange language and kissing him, or of the snug little house he was brought to as a newborn.

Once the greetings were over, I took Oliver by the hand and went down the tiled walkway past the yard where I had played with him on his blanket and hung his diapers, and told him about when he was a baby at this house. Ethel ran ahead of us, pointing out scenes of interest, such as the spot where she had seen the rat in the outdoor kitchen; the place under the bay tree where our dog, Tune, had attacked and killed one of the Fines' guinea fowl; and the creek where, looking for frogs with a friend, she had gotten soaking wet on a winter's day.

The acacia tree was just as I remembered it, but taller. In early June the bunches of white flowers were beginning to fade and dry, past their prime for dipping in batter and frying for the *beignets* I used to make. The kitchen where I had cooked so many meals was sooty and needed repainting, but in my mind's eye I could still see the wild herbs and drying strings of *sanguins* that I had hung in the corner near the woodstove when we had lived there.

Georgette called me back from my memories, shouting *"À table!"* and Donald came to get us. The Fines' familiar round green metal table, slightly rusted, was covered with a white embroidered cloth, and places were set for the six of us under the Virginia creeper that shaded their stone terrace. Georgette brought out a plate of pristine red and white radishes tipped with a few green leaves that she had pulled that morning from the garden, a plate of butter, and a small dish of salt. I silently promised myself I would buy radish seeds to take back to California and plant in our backyard. Denys followed with a basket of fresh bread, still warm from the bakery's late-morning bake, a bottle of red wine, and a carafe of water.

I had brushed against the sage near the table when I sat down, and its pungent fragrance hung in the air as we ate our first course, the crunchy radishes spread with just enough butter to hold the sprinkled salt. The wine, dark red and fruity, came from Taradeau, a neighboring village whose wine cooperative had a good reputation. After three years in exile in the Northern California bedroom community where we now lived, I felt that I had come home.

The wine was perfect with the bread and radishes, and went just as well with the hot, bubbling zucchini *gratin* that came next and the salad that followed. Denys brought out a second bottle to have with the cheese. Dessert was fresh figs.

It was the kind of meal that Provence is famous for, the reason, I think, that people travel to Provence, rent a house there, even buy a house and move, just to be part of the life of the Provençal table. Those long meals, composed of simple, fresh seasonal foods and local wines, savored under the cooling shade of sycamore or mulberry trees in warm weather and in front of a cozy fire in cold weather, are the essence of the good life, well lived.

So began our first summer back in Provence, when I would start to learn what it was like to live there as a summer vacationer, as part of the community but without the daily, arduous work of keeping goats and pigs. My days would be filled with food and cooking, long meals with friends and my family, and discovering the world that was to be part of me for the rest of my life.

We moved into the house we had bought just before our return to California. It had been replastered and painted, but still lacked indoor plumbing and electricity. We ran an electrical cord from Marie and Marcel Palazolli's place next door to ours, hauled water from the well, and built an outhouse. I unpacked the boxes of dishes, pots, books, toys, and photo albums that I brought with me from California when we first moved to Provence, and had packed away when we left, and I filled our pantry with food. We began to live again in Provence, this time on a long summer vacation.

....

Our social life, like everyone else's, revolved around food. We lingered over lunches and dinners, went to the open markets where we met friends for an *apéritif* or coffee, took picnics to the beaches and lakes, and went to restaurants and community feasts. We steeped ourselves in the tastes of Provence—olive oil, wild herbs, fish, tomatoes, eggplants, zucchini, grilled lamb and sausages, fresh cheese, and fruit of every kind.

138   In memory, it seems I spent at least part of almost every day cooking with my neighbors Marie, Georgette, Pascal, or Françoise. We all lived on the same road, a narrow, sinuous lane set in a small valley of unfenced vineyards, grain and melon fields, fruit orchards, and olive groves, punctuated by Marcel's vast market garden. Our days were subject only to the rhythm of nature and the table. It was natural for us all to pick cherries and peaches together from Marie and Marcel's trees, to help Françoise with the vats of tomato sauce she made to feed her children and grandchildren who came to spend much of the summer with her and Robert, to barbecue with Georgette and Denys, or to make elaborate dishes, like stuffed breast of veal, with Pascal.

Since Marie and I lived just a staircase apart, we saw each other throughout the day, and Donald and I sometimes helped her and Marcel with their farm tasks, such as pruning the melon vines, digging potatoes, or tying up tomato plants. Much of what I have learned over the years about growing food and cooking it came from my neighbors, especially Marie and Marcel, first during the years of our summer vacations and later as I continued to return. We often cooked and ate together and Marie always had something to show me or teach me.

That first summer back, I learned about the fish man.

He arrived every Thursday around 11:30, driving a small gray-blue Citroën van. He would honk his horn when he pulled in front of the farmhouse, and Marie and I would run down the stairs or in from the fields to meet him and buy something. She had been telling me we should get some sardines and cook them in my fireplace. Finally, the third week we were there he brought sardines. Marie came out the front door to the van just as I arrived from the tomato garden. The driver opened his sliding door to display the ice-packed shelf that sported an assortment of fish ranging from elegant and expensive *dorade* and sea bass to modest sardines and anchovies, plus a selection of fillets.

In the rural hinterlands of Provence, well into the 1970s and even later, it was common for purveyors of fish, meat, and dry goods to ply back roads like ours, bringing their products to the farms that dotted the countryside. Our weeks were structured by the arrival of the baker early every morning, the butcher on Sunday, and the fish man on Tuesday. The dry goods van came once a month. Their visits were highlighted by trips to the open markets, Wednesday in Aups, Saturday in Barjols, Sunday in Salernes, and to *épiceries,* or grocery stores. In those days, large supermarkets were far away in the cities, and the smaller versions of Intermarché and Casino that today serve medium-size villages had not yet been built. Most villages had only a tiny *épicerie*, maybe two. Some villages were too small to have even a weekly market, so the traveling purveyors were counted on to supply everything except fruits, vegetables, olive oil, and wine.

Country people, like all of my neighbors, had a *potager*, a kitchen garden, that provided vegetables daily throughout the year, plus fruit trees, olive trees, and grapevines. These supplied what the traveling vendors and *épiceries* did not. When the olives were harvested and then pressed at one of the olive oil mills, the farmer took his share of the oil, leaving a portion in payment for the milling, plus any excess that he wanted the mill to sell. He then got a fee per liter for his share when the rest of the oil was sold. The same was true with the grapes. They were delivered to the cooperative wineries, and once the grapes had been crushed and vinified, each farmer took back some wine for his own use, leaving the cooperative to sell the rest and pay him a return. Some farmers, including Marie and Marcel, kept rabbits and poultry in addition to a pig, so except for beef, seafood, bread, and dry goods, they and those like them were quite self-sufficient.

"Are they good and fresh?" Marie asked the fishmonger. "You know Marcel won't eat them if they're not."

"*Eh, ma belle, bien sûr!* Caught them myself this morning. You'll see. Freshest fish around. Look at those eyes! Still sharp, they are, bright and clear. A sure sign of a fresh fish."

Marie laughed, enjoying as she always did the chance to talk to someone from the outside. She extended the conversation as long as she dared. She loves to talk, and in the days before she and Marcel bought their own land and started selling their melons at the local markets, life could be lonely for her. I, too, loved both interacting with the vendors and being a part of the daily life of another culture. I knew that in just a few months I would be back in the classroom, teaching history and English to high-school students, eating a quick cheese sandwich, and grading papers during my thirty-minute lunch break. I reveled in the luxury of my French life, not a material luxury, but one of time and connections with the land and my neighbors that I didn't experience in California at that time.

I paid for our sardines and the fishmonger put them in brown paper bags and gave us some lemons. Marie took the fish and lemons upstairs to her refrigerator and we agreed to start the fire around seven that evening.

"I'll bring the wood and some grapevine prunings, and a grill," she said. "The fish are already cleaned. All we have to do is rub them with olive oil, a little salt, pepper, and some thyme. Won't take long."

It was going to be the first time I had cooked in our fireplace, and I was excited about it. The huge fireplace, gracefully sculpted in plaster, dominated one wall of the kitchen–living room. Oliver, at almost four years old, could stand upright in it. The hearth was deep, and its bricks jutted out onto the terracotta tiles of the floor. The mantel was broad, and when I stood on my tiptoes I could see the gleam of the glossy deep-red tiles covering its surface. My arms, outstretched, couldn't reach the far sides. When we bought the house, I had imagined what it might be like to cook in that fireplace. Tonight I would find out.

That afternoon, in preparation for the big evening, I made doughnuts for dessert, and Ethel helped. They were one of the few sweets I could prepare without an oven. For the first few summers we had only a two-burner propane cooktop that I kept on top of the *braise*, a waist-high structure made of stone and tile. In old Provençal kitchens, the *braise* was as important for cooking as the fireplace because it was here that the slow-cooking *daubes* and stews of wild boar, rabbit, lamb, or chicken simmered. Coals were scooped from the fireplace and placed on the tiled shelf beneath the square holes of the *braise*, and replenished as needed. The *braise* could also be used for quick cooking, such as frying or sautéing, by controlling the amount and heat of the coals.

When we renovated the house, the *braise* was dismantled, and the wall was smoothed with a new coating of plaster, leaving no trace of it except in my memory and in a few photographs. Those first summers, though, it was integral to all our meals, because it held the little cooktop.

I made doughnuts often during the summer, using a recipe from the gray cookbook, so-called for its cover, which I had brought with me from California when we first moved to France. A volume of more than a thousand pages, it was a gift from a family friend for my tenth birthday. My mother dismissed it, calling it too grown-up for a little girl, but that was exactly why I liked it. I still have the book, but the cover is long gone and the pages are frayed and stained. It's been my lifelong friend and has crossed the Atlantic Ocean twice and survived many moves. Even now, I keep it on a shelf in my California kitchen and turn to it for my favorite brownie recipe or a quick reference on how to make a fresh cherry pie.

From it, I taught Ethel to make raised doughnuts, one of my childhood favorites. That day Ethel kneaded the dough on the wooden trestle table in the middle of the large room. After greasing a bowl with lard—true lard that Marie had rendered during the winter when she and Marcel slaughtered the annual pig—we put our dough in it, covered it with a cloth, then set it on the red-tiled windowsill to rise. When the dough was ready, we rolled it out on the floured table and used upturned glasses to cut circles. Sometimes we used knives instead and cut squares of random and irregular sizes, just for fun.

Ethel, who was then just about the same age as I was when I made my first doughnuts, especially liked the frying part. We heated chunks of white lard in her great-grandmother's cast-iron Dutch oven that had made the journey first from Texas, then to California, then to France. When the fat was hot, Ethel, standing on a small stool, slid in the cut-out dough. "Watch out," I said, hovering behind her, wanting to let her do it herself, but also afraid she would be splattered by the hot fat.

"I can do it. I won't get burnt."

"Here, let me turn them."

"OK, but I get to take them out."

I turned the doughnuts, and when the other side was brown, Ethel lifted them onto plates lined with the paper bags we saved from stores. When all the doughnuts were done, we put them, still warm, in a fresh paper bag and shook them with sugar, sampled a few, then called Oliver and Donald inside to try them.

As promised, Marie appeared a little before seven. Our doughnuts were tucked away, ready to serve. I had set the table ahead of time, and put out *pastis*, water, and olives. I wanted to be free to cook in the fireplace with Marie.

"I love fires," Marie said as she carefully stacked twigs and then larger pieces of oak in an ever-rising bed on the fireplace hearth. She then lit the bottommost twigs.

"They keep you company. You tend them, take care of them, and they reward you with warmth and companionship."

Marie and Marcel didn't have a fireplace, and I suspected that for many years before we bought our piece of the big *mas*, they cooked in what was now our fireplace and then took the food upstairs to their kitchen. Tonight we'd eat in front of the fireplace, something I was sure they'd never done. The month of June had been a cool one so far, and a fire would not be unwelcome.

I had a *pastis* and Marie had *menthe l'eau*, and we chatted while we watched the oak burn down, poking and adjusting the fire until we had a bed of hot coals. Then we threw on the *sarments,* the grape prunings. They smoldered briefly before bursting into flame and perfuming the air. It was time to position the grilling rack on the bricks we had arranged earlier. Everyone was at the table now. Donald and Marcel were having a *pastis* and eating olives, and Oliver, Ethel, and Aileen, Marie and Marcel's daughter, sipped on grenadine drinks and ate peanuts. Florent, their son, now fourteen and studying English in school, was trying out words such as "feesh" and "waater" on Ethel and

Oliver, while they laughed hysterically at his pronunciation, trying to get him to say "fish" and "water" instead.

Marie and I, hunkered by the fire, did the cooking. The slippery sardines went from their olive oil marinade onto the grill, where they quickly sizzled golden on one side and their eyes turned opaque, before we flipped them over. We grilled the fish in batches, filling a platter and sitting down to eat that batch before cooking another. At first I was carefully cutting and lifting the small fillet from each of the sardines on my plate until Marcel said, "Just pick it up and eat it. Like this." He held a fish in two hands, like corn on the cob, and ate all but the head and tail.

"Like that," he said, discarding the remains and picking up another fish, squeezing lemon over it before starting in. I have since witnessed this traditional style of eating sardines many times, none more impressive than at village *sardinades*, sardine feasts, where hundreds of people sit down at community tables to eat their fill of fish hot off the grill, drink wine, and socialize.

Sardines are one of the most important of the Mediterranean fisheries, and the Provençals have devised any number of ways to eat them. Besides being grilled, still my favorite way to eat them, they are also used to make a special *bouillabaisse* and a variety of souplike dishes. Sometimes they are boned and stuffed with fillings ranging from mussels and fish dumplings to spinach and parsley. They're cooked in white wine, red wine, poached, baked, or fried. They're combined with vegetables in jellied molds, whipped into *pâtés*, and molded into *timbales*. An accommodating little fish, the sardine is inexpensive, plentiful, and certainly versatile.

The children loved the usually forbidden idea of eating with their hands, and we snacked off the meat, imitating Marcel, leaving the head, tail, and bone behind, like a cat's meal in a cartoon.

Bread and wine were copious, and at last, when there were no longer any fish, we gathered up the dishes and platters of bones and stacked them on the sink while Marcel set to slicing and passing out the sweet, honey-flavored Charentais melon he had brought with him. Ethel carried our sugar doughnuts to the table and I poured espresso into small white cups as the coals glimmered and darkened. Satiated and happy, we decided to leave the dishes until the morning, and we all went up to our respective beds, shutting the kitchen door behind us.

....

That summer, and all the summers and years to follow, I cooked mostly out of my neighbors' gardens and orchards, especially Marie and Marcel's, and, as often as I could, in the fireplace. Marcel was, and still is, the best vegetable and fruit grower around. Even now, in his mid-seventies, he plants more vegetables than he and all his relatives and neighbors can possibly eat, or than he can sell at the morning markets he and Marie still faithfully attend, as much for the sociability as for the income. You can always spot them—no elaborate refrigerated van, brightly colored retractable awnings, or cash register, just a modest folding table; crates of melons, tomatoes, green beans, asparagus, or peaches, whatever is in season for them; a small metal cash box; and a scale.

At any market in Provence one is sure to find people like Marie and Marcel selling the fruits and vegetables they grow themselves. Their day starts early, sometimes beginning with picking. Next they load their small trucks with the boxes of produce and tables, maybe an umbrella, and drive fifteen to seventy or more kilometers away and set up at the marketplace. By noon, if all goes well, their products are sold, and it's time to pack up, go home for lunch, have a nap, and go back to work in their fields and orchards.

Some markets, called *marchés paysans,* are devoted exclusively to vendors who grow everything they sell, often *biologique,* or organic. In most markets, such vendors are mixed among others who are resellers of purchased fruits and vegetables. Producers like Marie and Marcel are often distinguished by their modest stalls, while the resellers' stalls have far more elaborate setups that often include lights as well as ample awnings and banks of shelves holding the produce, often not locally grown. At the stalls of the artisanal vendors selling only their own produce, much of it shows variation in shape, size, and color because whatever is ripe is sold. The reseller vendors buy from large farming operations or brokers where products are sorted for uniform size and color before packing and shipping.

Marcel's tomatoes, for example, are an heirloom variety he has grown for years from seeds that initially came from an uncle who brought them from Italy. They are big, round, and broad at the bottom with grooves that rise to narrow shoulders and a nearly pointed top. The dark red hue fades to green at the shoulders. Compared to the perfectly calibrated tomatoes from large-scale production in Holland and Spain, neatly packed in regular rows in specially designed cartons, Marcel's tomatoes, stacked into his recycled wooden crates, look like an altogether different fruit. However, as soon as he arrives at the market, customers who know the flavor of his tomatoes line up to buy them, just as they do his melons, or his asparagus, or whatever else he is selling.

Since I first met Marie and Marcel, they have told me to help myself to whatever I wanted from their gardens, so that is what I have done. What a luxury! During those early summers with the children, when gardening and homegrown vegetables were still new to me, I reveled in picking shiny purple eggplants, perfectly ripe tomatoes, dark green zucchini, and long sweet red peppers to prepare *ratatouille* as Marie taught me. I made tomato *coulis* under her instruction as well, cooking Marcel's tomatoes down to a thick sauce with garlic, onion, and basil. The beans, whose vines climbed up tepees made from tree branches Marcel gathered from the forest, were long and fat, the best I had ever eaten. These, too, he grew from seeds originally from Italy, saving them every year just as he did the tomato seeds and melon seeds. The potatoes, all dug at once over a day or two in July, usually with me and Donald helping, were kept in Marie and Marcel's *cave* along with onions and garlic, and I was welcome to those as well.

147

A favorite summer dish was simply potatoes cooked with beans until the beans were falling-apart tender, seasoned with salt, pepper, and *sarriette*, the winter savory that grows wild in high places. We followed the seasons with Marcel's fruit, beginning with cherries in early June; moving on to apricots, peaches, plums, and melons; and, just before returning to California in late August, figs.

That first summer back in Provence, Marie also taught me how to cook some of her favorite dishes, including *petits farcis*. I now teach this dish to the students who come to my cooking school, after first taking them to one of the open markets to meet Marie and Marcel and buy the vegetables we need.

Marcel is from Nice, and *petits farcis* are a summer specialty of that city, although they are found all over Provence. Marie had learned how to make them from his Niçoise aunt, and that was the method she taught me. She began by scooping out halves of small eggplants, round zucchini, sweet peppers, and tomatoes. She finely minced the pulp of the eggplant and zucchini and seeded and chopped the tomato flesh. These all went into a bowl with a mixture of sausage and slices of a day-old *baguette* soaked in and swelling with milk. The mixture was seasoned with finely minced onion and garlic, parsley, thyme, salt, and pepper, and bound together with an egg or two, then mounded into the vegetable shells.

Marie explained to me that now she cooks the *petits farcis* in her oven, but before she had an oven, she cooked them on top of the stove.

"I still do it that way sometimes. They get a crunchier crust," she told me one day as she poured a thin film of olive oil over the bottom of a large frying pan. She placed the stuffed vegetables in the oil, stuffing-side up, and cooked them gently for about ten minutes. "Now watch. This is Tatie's trick." Using a spatula and with a little help from her fingers, she turned the stuffed vegetables and gently cooked them until the stuffing was browned, something I would never have thought of doing. She turned them again, covered them with a lid, and cooked them another twenty minutes or so. The tomatoes were done a little sooner, so she took them out first.

Petits farcis became a summer standard for us. I made them hot for dinner or lunch, or I packed them to eat at room temperature for picnics at Quinson, Bauduen, or Esparron, the lakes where we went swimming almost every day after working on the house or going to the markets. When we did our own version of potluck with Adèle and Pascal, which we did frequently, Pascal cooked the main dish and I brought a first course, like *petits farcis*.

Pascal and Adèle, both in their very early twenties and still at university, spent summers at his parents' vacation house down the road from us, and we saw them often. Pascal loved to eat good food and to cook, just like his father. Over the years, we've cooked side by side many times, stuffing the fresh fish he caught in the rivers, making rich dark sauces with wild mushrooms I brought from excursions to the mountains, or preparing *gratins* of fennel or spinach with vegetables from Marcel's garden.

....

My memories of those long, hot summers in Provence are mapped by water, when the geography of our days was drawn according to the rivers and lakes where we swam and played. Each of our swimming spots was associated with food.

149

In the relatively small part of Provence where we spent our summers, the inland waters are dominated by the Verdon River. The Verdon originates in the Maritime Alps and flows southwest, first through a deep, picturesque canyon, the Gorges du Verdon, then through the *département* of the Var before it joins the Durance River. In the early 1970s, the Verdon was dammed into several lakes for irrigation and drinking water and for hydroelectic power.

The Lac de Quinson was the closest to us, ten minutes from our house. The lake, not much more than a long, wide spot in the river, was created in 1975 when a series of dams was built along the Verdon and the water overflowed a deep, narrow gorge and covered part of the Plain de Quinson. The shore of the newly formed "beach" at Quinson was still dotted with willow trees and wild grasses and had the ruins of a small *cabanon*, or cottage. We would try to get a shady spot under one of the trees where we would lay our beach mats, unfold our aluminum beach chairs, and prop our picnic basket against the trunk.

Our picnics were simple—olives, fresh *baguettes*, *La vache qui rit* cheese (Oliver's favorite), Camembert, slices of ham, chocolate, and some fruit. We brought water or Oranginas for Ethel and Oliver, red wine for Donald and me. Sometimes I made a tomato salad with bits of red onion and a thick, garlicky vinaigrette. We dipped pieces of bread into the salad juices, then topped the bread with cheese or ham, or both, to make a sandwich. The plates were eventually wiped clean with the bread, packed back in the basket, and taken home to be washed.

A day at the lake at Quinson always included a visit to the waterside *café* opposite the beach. Before heading for home, we walked up to the road and across the bridge to take seats in the heavy shade of the mulberry trees that lined the *café* terrace overlooking the lake. The road separated the bar and *café* interior from the terrace. We watched the waiter as he crossed the road to the terrace to take our order, and after Donald and I had ordered our espressos, one of us would cross the road with Ethel and Oliver so they could choose an ice cream from the deep cooler in the *café*.

Once or twice during the summer we would come back to the *café* at night to eat its thin-crusted pizzas, topped with homemade tomato sauce and olives and either cheese, anchovies, or mushrooms, and cooked in the wood-fired oven. The lake, our playground of the afternoon, was slate-tinged silver if the moon was out, inky black if it wasn't. The metal tables, bare when we had our coffee and ice cream, were covered with red-and-white plaid cotton tablecloths overlaid with white butcher paper, and the sparkling fairy lights strung in the trees were lit. We'd order a carafe of *rosé*, Oranginas for Ethel and Oliver, and pizzas for each of us.

Our favorite place to go for a special meal became Le Relais Notre-Dame, just down the road from the *café*. It sits on the curve where the road begins to climb to the plateau of Riez. There is no view of the lake, only of the fields of wheat and barley farmed nearly to the edge of the water, but from the restaurant's terrace we could feel the presence of the lake and smell the water.

In those days, two generations, the grandfather and his daughter and her husband, worked at the hotel and its restaurant, while their children, young then, played on the edges of the dining room or a corner of the terrace. Like the *café,* Le Relais Notre-Dame was on both sides of the road, with tables on a terrace shaded by plane trees on one side, the hotel and restaurant, with their old-fashioned façade and gardens on the other side.

151

The Brunos had told us about the restaurant, as they had told us about so many things.

"You must go there," M. Bruno insisted. "The Provençal food they serve is perfect, all prepared right there by the family. Completely authentic. Monsieur Devoe, the grandfather, and his wife—she's dead now—bought it after World War I. He was injured in the war and still limps. In those days, it was before the automobile, or when the automobile was still a novelty— remember, until the 1940s, some of these places in the back-country didn't even have roads.

"The hotel," M. Bruno continued, "was also a stop for the *diligence,* the stagecoaches that were the main source of trans-portation here. Have you read Jean Giono's books? He lived in Manosque and wrote about Haute Provence and the life in the villages and the isolated farms during those years, right until he died just a few years ago. They'll give you an idea of life in the times of the *diligence,* especially Giono's *Regain.*"

I made a note to get the book, which I eventually did. I loved it. The haunting picture Giono painted of life in Haute-Provence at the beginning of the nineteenth century enriched the landscape for me, giving it depth and context. Never again was I able to look at a roadside, turn-of-the-century hotel like Le Relais Notre-Dame without peopling it with horses, carriages, and characters from *Regain.* His other books only reinforced my sense of the history of the land and the place.

"Now, when you go to Notre-Dame you'll notice that there is a very tall, wide garage on one side. That was to allow the coaches and horses to enter. Ah, but we were talking about the food. They cure their own hams, make their own *pâté* and *caillettes*, and even make their own *pieds-et-paquets*. They keep a *potager*, a big one, and cook out of it every day. If you want fresh fish, there's a trout pond in the back, fed by the Verdon. You won't get better, fresher food anywhere." We had to try it.

When we first went, I was somewhat intimidated. It was far more formal than anywhere we were used to eating, and very, very quiet. It was a rather cool night in June, and although a few people were having *apéritifs* on the terrace, dinner was being served only inside. Stepping into the restaurant, we found ourselves in a foyer of sorts, created by a full-length wood and zinc bar on one side and a row of potted plants on the other. Beyond the plants we could see the dining room tables set with gleaming silver and heavy, starched white linens, framed by floor-to-ceiling peach-colored satin curtains, tied back with thick gold cords set against peach wallpaper. The walls were decorated with oil paintings in gilded frames. Most of the tables were taken.

"*Bonsoir.*" We were greeted by a youngish woman dressed simply in a beige skirt and white blouse. "Are you here for dinner?" she asked, looking at Ethel and Oliver and smiling. "Yes," Donald replied. I recognized her as one of the women I had seen coming and going along the road from the garden.

I was nervous because I was uncertain if our children would be able to sustain their table manners during what would inevitably be at least an hour and a half in a sedate dining situation. I was glad when we were seated near a window toward the rear of the dining room. Oliver had brought his current favorite GI Joes, and Ethel had a Barbie doll along with several changes of doll clothes and a Nancy Drew book. Thus far they were enjoying the novelty of eating in such a fancy restaurant and were particularly interested in the several diners who had their dogs with them, perched on chairs or curled under their owners' feet.

We ordered *pastis* and, for Ethel and Oliver, *limonade au grenadine*, then perused the menu. Abruptly, a rear door opened not far from us, and a tall, stooped man in brown pants and a maroon sweater-vest made his way across the dining room with the good part of a whole ham dangling from one hand, a basket of greens in the other, and a bottle of wine tucked under each arm. I was thrilled to see him, because when M. Bruno had told us about him, I had immediately invested this elderly man with a romantic past, historically linked to the food and the land.

"Look," I whispered, "that must be the owner, the grandfather that M. Bruno told us about." We watched him as he made his way across the room, slowly and deliberately, not looking to either side. He had a large nose and a thick thatch of silver hair. "Remember, he told us they cured their own hams." We got a glimpse of the kitchen as he went through a set of swinging doors.

In the old days, the *rélais* and small hotels where the *diligences* stopped were essentially self-sufficient, growing and providing the food not only for the passengers but for the animals. The *diligence,* a coach pulled by a team of horses, varied in size, with the largest carrying up to twenty passengers inside three compartments and as much as a thousand kilos, more than two thousand pounds, of baggage. Although Quinson was small, only a few hundred people at the turn of the century, it had been an important stop on the route linking the coast to Digne and the high Alpine valleys and to the interior region of Manosque and Forcalquier, west of the Durance River.

153

The *rélais* were often associated, through the extended family of the owners, with large, diversified farms so that the food at the inns followed the same food patterns as those of the local farm families. *Charcuterie* was produced from their own pigs, fresh meat was supplied for the hungry travelers from the chickens, rabbits, lambs, sheep, and squab the family raised, and wild birds and game were hunted in the nearby forests. Milk and cheese came from a few goats and sheep kept for that purpose, and vegetables were grown year-round in the *potager*, supplemented by asparagus, leeks, mushrooms, and snails gathered in the wild.

Cavernous kitchens held stoves and ovens fired by wood, and *braises* that could support large, deep pans of simmering stews or water. Olives, wine, olive oil, potatoes, onions, and nuts were stored in *caves*. Curing meats, hanging from hooks, were kept in well-ventilated rooms that maintained constant low temperatures.

As late as the 1990s, until the European norms on food safety became increasingly strict and strictly enforced, places like Le Relais Notre-Dame still followed the patterns set down in the early days. The food was, as a matter of course, fresh, artisanal, and seasonal. In fall, the restaurant would serve homemade *saucissons*, *pâtés*, and *daubes* made of wild boar. Wild *chanterelles* and *cèpes,* purchased at the kitchen's back door from friends or gathered by the family, appeared in *omelettes* and sauces. In winter, truffles, found or purchased clandestinely, were standard fare, and in January, as soon as one of the family pigs was slaughtered, fresh pork and blood sausages would be on the menu. Come spring, asparagus, morel mushrooms, lamb, young peas and fava beans, and artichokes dominated.

Our first dinner at Le Relais Notre-Dame was memorable for its simplicity and flavors, and for the fact that Ethel and Oliver remained interested throughout the meal, never complaining, always looking forward to what would come next. We ordered three *prix-fixe* three-course menus, and a main dish *à la carte* for Oliver, plus a carafe of red wine. I chose the *crudité* plate for a first course, Ethel and Donald the *charcuterie*, planning on sharing among the four of us. The *charcuterie* platter for three was laden with scoops of homemade *pâté* straight from the preserving jar, with just a little of the fat from the top, *jambon cru*, sliced, I am sure, from the ham that had just passed through the dining room, rounds of *saucisson* very similar to Marcel's, and slices of what we called regular ham as opposed to salt-cured *jambon cru*. A crock of butter and a sprinkling of green and black olives and little *cornichons* completed the platter.

The *crudité* platter was smaller, but amply furnished with my favorite *carottes rapées*, or grated carrot salad, plus slices of new potatoes drizzled with olive oil and parsley, summer tomatoes, and cucumbers. The tomatoes were sprinkled with a little minced garlic, the cucumbers with just salt, pepper, and olive oil. Each different small salad was mounded on its own lettuce leaf, and the whole plate was garnished with black olives. A basket of sliced *baguette* came to the table as well.

The platters were almost too beautiful to disturb, but we divided the *charcuterie* and the *crudités* among us. We slathered our bread with butter (it's the only time you have butter at a French table, except with radishes and sea salt) and added *saucisson,* ham, or *pâté*, making each bite extra rich. I can still close my eyes and taste that first course all over again.

The *pâté* was a little creamier than Marie and Marcel's, and when I eventually came to know the owners of Notre-Dame and to talk with them about their food, they told me that they used a grinder to make the *pâté*, and a smaller quantity of liver than was usual, adding more meat and fat instead, and seasoned it with their own *eau-de-vie*, at least as long as their grandfather was alive. His generation was the last to have the legal right to make distilled products, like *eau-de-vie*, in this case an eighty-proof alcohol made from distilling the skins and seeds of the grapes after pressing.

Ethel ordered fresh trout that first night at Le Relais. She loved that the trout were swimming just behind the hotel in a specially built pond. Oliver had his usual steak and potatoes, and Donald and I had the *plat du jour*, rabbit cooked with tomatoes and eggplant, accompanied by the same chunky fried potatoes served with Ethel's fish and Oliver's meat. The rabbit, served in a brown earthenware casserole for two, fell from the bone in tender chunks. Summer's tomatoes and eggplant were intensely flavored and seasoned with garlic and sprigs of wild thyme. We shared bites with one another, and Donald and I agreed that Ethel's fish was exquisite, Oliver's steak juicy and perfectly cooked.

We finished our meal with a strawberry *charlotte,* a sort of French trifle, with cream and fresh berries and cake made in a special *charlotte* mold. The restaurant sent a little dish of fresh strawberry ice cream for Ethel and Oliver while we had an espresso, lingering over the meal as long as possible.

From that night on, we made a point to have at least one lunch or dinner at Le Relais every summer, a habit that I maintained after we no longer came as a family. The grandfather is gone, and the son too, and now Le Relais is run by the grandchildren, Denys and Monique, neither of whom are married. They purchase their *charcuterie*, except for a house-made *pâté*, and buy their wild mushrooms, truffles, and game from wholesale vendors, so the food is different, but still in the same familial style and sensibility.

Denys learned to cook from his mother, who was the cook when we first went there. He still makes his mother's *charlotte*, changing it with the season. In fall he uses chestnuts, in summer peaches and berries, and in winter chocolate. Rabbit stew appears periodically, along with other traditional dishes such as *ratatouille,* and some more modern ones that reflect convenience rather than the rhythms of farm life.

The *potager* that served the kitchen so well was dug up and replaced with a swimming pool for the hotel guests. The last of the vegetable beds is devoted to flower beds brimming with dahlias in the summer, but the trout pond is still there. 157

Some years I take my cooking school students to Le Relais Notre-Dame, and we have an *apéritif* in the walled rose garden behind the kitchen. I show them the trout pond, actually a large, deep cement basin, at the far edge of the garden under a willow tree. Often during our *apéritif,* Denys emerges from the kitchen with a long net and heads for the pond, where in a flash he scoops up a plump trout and heads back to the kitchen. He cooks it to order, either *à la meunière,* in butter, or fried in olive oil.

....

One of my best memories of long summer meals was a meal that took place in a village square at midnight on Bastille Day. A group of us, including Joanne and Guild, who lived and worked in Paris, but came down frequently to their house in Provence, went together. Pascal proposed the adventure, saying we should all go to Entrecasteaux for *soupe au pistou* at midnight to celebrate Bastille Day on July 14, the French independence day named after the infamous prison whose fall symbolized the end of the French monarchy and the beginning of the French Republic. Like the Fourth of July in the United States, the occasion is marked by fireworks and varied celebrations, most of them including food.

Pascal had a summer job doing masonry work in Entrecasteaux and while working there met the owner of one of the small restaurants on the village square. She was putting on a special meal for Bastille Day—bottomless bowls of *soupe au pistou*, wine, and bread for twenty francs, children under twelve half-price. It sounded like fun, so we all decided to go. I had heard about the village, and even though it was only twenty minutes away, I had never been to it.

When we arrived at nine, it was still light and the great block of the *château* in the heart of the village cast mauve shadows across its gardens. The *château* gardens were designed by André Le Nôtre, the renowned "gardener of the kings of France," and were patterned after the gardens at Versailles. First built in the thirteenth century on the ruins of an eleventh-century fort, then rebuilt in the sixteenth century, the *château* had housed a series of nobles, some who had come to bitter ends. The *château* was taken from the family during the French Revolution, but was eventually returned to them, and they owned it until 1949, when it became part of the property of the *commune*. The *château* and gardens, fully restored, are considered one of the most important intact examples of *château*-fortress architecture in Provence. They made a dramatic setting for fireworks and feasts to celebrate Bastille Day.

Once we arrived on the square, Pascal went to see his friend, Anik, to reserve seats for us at one of the long tables laid out in front of her restaurant. The tables were covered in the white butcher paper, standard table dressing for community feasts, and were decorated with jars of flowers and small French flags. Unlabeled wine bottles of red and *rosé* were already out on the tables, and spoons and bowls were set at each place, even though the soup wouldn't be served for at least another hour or so. When he came back, Pascal told us that Anik and her helpers were a little overwhelmed in the kitchen, having discovered they were short of the ovenproof casseroles they were using to serve the soup. He slipped two pieces of paper with *reservée 8 personnes* written on them under two of the wine bottles about midway down one of the tables. People had already been draping sweaters and jackets over the backs of some of the chairs or tilting them forward to indicate those seats were taken. We tilted our eight chairs, then set out to wander through the village.

Fairy lights glittered in the sycamore trees that lined the squares and already we could hear firecrackers being set off in the narrow streets, competing for attention with the rasping of the cicadas. By the time we returned, the tables were filling up and children were running and playing in the square, waiting until the food was served to join their families at the tables. Ethel and Oliver hung around the edge of the square, watching the children from the shadows.

The night was warm, with just a soft riffle of air. The women wore dresses with thin straps, showing off recently acquired tans, and most of the men were in loose, short-sleeved shirts, or T-shirts, with a few wearing what I call white underwear shirts, the sleeveless cotton undershirt that Marlon Brando wore in *A Streetcar Named Desire*. The heat was still rising from the cobblestones beneath us, and no one needed the sweaters or jackets brought along just in case.

As the first huge bowls of soup came from the kitchen and were set down along the middle of the tables, people began to cheer and to lift their wineglasses in toasts.

"Vive la France! Vive la pistou!" "La Marseillaise," the national anthem of the French Revolution, poured at high volume from loudspeakers mounted on the roof of the *mairie,* the city hall, next door, and everyone started singing along and clinking their glasses, toasting in step with the rousing music. Even though I

didn't know the words and certainly can't sing, I found myself caught up in the toasting across and down the length of the table, and I vowed I'd learn the words so next time I could at least pretend I was singing. I clinked glasses as far as I could reach in all directions. By the time the song was over, all the tables had been served with soup and people settled down to eat against a backdrop of the village-sponsored fireworks.

Pascal ladled the soup for our group into the shallow soup bowls, each spoonful enfolding us with the steamy aroma of garlic and basil. When he handed me my bowl, I could see the plumped beans and zucchini beneath the nearly creamy broth and the brilliant green *pistou* sauce swirled across the top of the soup. It tasted of summer, and we ate it by the bowlful, dipping our bread into it and adding more *pistou*.

The *pistou*, a sauce added just before serving, is akin to Italian pesto. It worked its way into the canon of Provençal cooking by way of Nice, which didn't become a part of France until 1860. Pesto's origins are thought to be the Ligurian coast of Italy, just east of Nice, but the Niçoise version, which has spread through-out Provence, has no pine nuts. Pine nuts are considered essential to Italian pesto but are anathema to classic Provençal *pistou*. In general it begins with sea salt and garlic crushed in a mortar to make a paste, then handfuls of basil leaves are added and crushed as well. The sauce is finished with olive oil and enough Gruyère or Parmesan, or a combination of the two, to make a thick sauce that is later thinned with a little soup broth. Some versions include the pulp of a small tomato, and I've read recipes that omit the garlic, though to me that would be unimaginable.

The soup itself is vegetable and the ingredients vary, but the essential element is the fresh *coco blanc* or *coco rouge* shelling bean, available only in summer or early fall, when you see them, still in their pods, heaped in the market stalls. The white ones are in pale yellow pods, and the beans themselves are ivory colored. *Coco rouge* beans are pale tan with streaks of maroon, and their pods are brilliant carmine with white mottling.

The more aggressive market vendors call out, *"Cocos! Cocos pour la bonne soupe au pistou! Ici, ici les bons cocos."* In my experience, *soupe au pistou* always has green beans, either thin, delicate *haricots verts fin* or long, flat *mange-touts*, or both. Zucchini, carrots, onions, leeks, potatoes, sometimes turnips, sometimes tomatoes, plus sea salt and pepper, and maybe pasta, complete the mix. The vegetables are cooked in succession, beginning with the *cocos* and the onions, which are brought to a boil in a large pot of water and simmered for about twenty minutes. Next come the other vegetables, chopped or diced, along with branches of thyme, and the soup is simmered another fifteen minutes. Finally, when the vegetables are tender, a handful of pasta, such as broken spaghetti or small macaroni, is added, along with salt and pepper to taste. Once the pasta is soft—no *al dente* here—the *pistou* is added. The soup is served accompanied by extra *pistou* and extra grated cheese.

That night at Entrecasteaux we ate our fill of *soupe au pistou*. As soon as the communal bowl was empty, a waiter or waitress brought a full one, then another, on into the night. Full wine bottles kept replacing empty ones, and baskets of bread never ended. It was after midnight before the apple tart arrived, and by then Oliver was asleep, his head in my lap. It was just chilly enough to put on the sweater I had brought, and the cicadas were less insistent in the cooling night. The teenagers had taken over the cobbled streets, setting off firecrackers, while the adults were starting to head home.

Soupe au pistou

VEGETABLE SOUP WITH BASIL-GARLIC SAUCE

My friend Anne, who is from Marseille, taught me this version of the quintessential summer and early fall soup of Provence, so thick with fresh shelling beans and vegetables that a wooden spoon can almost stand up straight in it. Just before serving, the soup is laced with the *pistou*, a *purée* of garlic, basil, and olive oil.

B egin by putting 2 quarts water in a soup pot. Add a teaspoon of coarse sea salt, three handfuls of green beans (each cut into several pieces), and a handful of diced carrot. Next, dice the following vegetables and add them to the pot: three small potatoes, a couple of medium zucchini, and a small onion. Finally, add three handfuls of fresh shelling beans, such as *cocos rouges*, cranberry beans, or *cocos blancs*, white beans. Add several pinches of fresh thyme and a bay leaf.

Bring the water to a rolling boil, then reduce the heat and simmer until all the vegetables are soft and the liquid has reduced by about one-third. Allow about 40 minutes for this. Taste the soup and add more salt, plus freshly ground black pepper and more herbs if needed. Add a handful of spaghetti broken into small pieces, and continue to cook until the pasta is tender, about another 10 minutes.

While the soup is simmering, put three or four cloves of coarsely chopped garlic in a mortar and add a pinch of coarse sea salt. With a pestle, grind the salt and garlic until it becomes a creamy paste. Add a handful of basil and crush until blended with the paste. Add another handful of leaves and crush these. Now, slowly drizzle in about 1/3 cup extra-virgin olive oil and, still using the pestle, incorporate the oil until a thick green sauce, the *pistou*, has formed. Allow 10 to 15 minutes to make the *pistou*.

When the soup is ready, put it into a terrine or large bowl. Stir in about half of the *pistou*, reserving the rest to accompany the soup.

SERVES 4 TO 6

CHAPTER 6

THE ESSENCE OF GARLIC
AND LE GRAND AÏOLI

The garlic gap. Oil and garlic, a perfect marriage. Forty cloves and
a chicken. Snails in prehistory. Discovering salt cod.

Garlic in Provence is taken very seriously, and if a single ingredient could be said to be essential to Provençal cooking, it would
be garlic. It's surprisingly versatile in both its taste and its uses.
Searingly pungent when raw, it becomes increasingly mild the
longer it is cooked, and distinctly mellow when slowly roasted.
Omnipresent year-round in every Provençal kitchen, garlic is
used to season everything from salads to soups, stews, and sautés,
and is a required ingredient for making such famous Provençal
dishes as *aïoli, tapenade, anchoïdade,* and *brandade de morue.*

There is one small problem, however. A month-long gap
exists after the previous year's crop has run its course and before
the arrival of the new crop of mature garlic at the market. The
Provençal garlic farmer's solution to this gap is to sell part of the
crop as *l'ail jeune,* young garlic, thus allowing everyone to have
garlic in their kitchens without a break. *L'ail jeune* lasts only a

month or so before deteriorating, while the papery-skinned mature garlic can be stored for months. When young garlic is harvested, the head of cloves has completely formed, but the skin surrounding it is still moist and supple. To produce mature garlic for storage, the bulbs are left in the ground for another month or so until the leaves droop and die. The bulbs are pulled and then cured in a dry place.

Young garlic is eagerly awaited in Provence, and people have come to look forward to it much as they anticipate the first asparagus or strawberries, knowing the crop will be in season for only a short time. Sometime in May, vendors start bringing truckloads of young garlic—white, red, or purple depending upon the variety—braided, tied in bunches, or as loose heads with a bit of the stalk intact. For several weeks the neatly arranged stacks of young garlic scent the air of the open markets. I usually buy a braid, which has a dozen heads, and hang it in my kitchen, taking a head as needed. I cook with young garlic just as I would with mature garlic, but the flavor of the young bulb is milder, its cloves bright white and crunchy, with no hint of the yellowing or sprouting that comes with age. One dish that I make only with young garlic is a salad of arugula and *frisée* generously dressed with a vinaigrette of minced garlic, parsley, olive oil, sea salt, and vinegar. The sprightly, faintly earthy taste of the just-dug garlic is inimitable in the dressing and can't be replicated with mature garlic.

By the time the one or two heads left on my braid of young garlic have started to soften and mold, the new harvest of cured garlic has arrived at the market; I bring home a braid and hang it on the same peg near the stove. I also buy cured garlic in a bunch and hang it on the other side of the stove. I love the way the bunch looks, fat whitish brown bulbs gathered together at the neck with a wire, the dry leaves twisting and curling in every direction. The bunch of garlic is as beautiful in its way as a bouquet of wildflowers or lavender.

The arrival of the new crop of garlic is the time to make the famous *poulet aux quarante gousses d'ail,* chicken with forty cloves of garlic. The cloves, which are cooked *en chemise,* with their skin on, are reduced to a soft paste during the nearly two hours that the chicken roasts. When ready, the chicken is carved and served along with its juices and the cloves, and the lucky diners squeeze the mellow paste from the softened cloves onto their bread. The better the quality of the garlic, the better the flavor and quality of the paste, which is what makes this dish so special. The first time I read this recipe I was unable to imagine eating anything that contained forty cloves of garlic, but I wanted to try it. It was shortly after we renovated our Provençal kitchen, in 1979, and for the first time, I had a standard stove with a full-size oven. *Poulet aux quarante gousses d'ail* was one of the first dishes I made, and it immediately became a summer favorite. I used nearly four bulbs of garlic for that one dish! Once, we even went to the huge garlic fair in Marseille to buy our summer supply of the pungent bulb.

Garlic is so important in Provence that there is a month-long garlic fair in Marseille whose origins date to the fifteenth century. From the middle of June to the middle of July every year, garlic vendors man stalls set along the Cours Belsunce, a major street that crosses the grand Canebière in the heart of the old city. Here you can find multiple garlic varieties, white, red, and pink, now fully mature, in bulk, braids, or bunches. People come to the fair from all over the region to buy their garlic. Provisioning themselves for the coming year, they make sure they have plenty of garlic in the *cave* to make *aïoli, anchoïade, pistou,* and *poulet aux quarante gousses d'ail,* to season legs of lamb, to rub on toasts, to

167

sauté with onions and vegetables, and to make soups and stews. *Aïoli* is arguably the most famous garlic dish of Provence, and it gives it name to an entire meal—*le grand aïoli.*

168

To make *aïoli*, garlic cloves are firmly crushed into a paste with sharp-edged crystals of coarse sea salt. The crushed garlic is whisked together with egg yolks, then olive oil is slowly added and the mixture is whisked until it becomes a luminous, golden green mayonnaise, fragrant and pungent with garlic. The Provençaux eat the condiment with meats, fish, and shellfish and use it as a spread, but it is *le grand aïoli* that celebrates its namesake. *Le grand aïoli* consists of platters and bowls laden with cooked vegetables and fish, and sometimes snails, accompanied by vast bowls of *aïoli*. This festive meal is often served at large family gatherings. In earlier times, when hard, long days of farmwork were the norm, it was the heart of *les fêtes campagnardes*, rural celebrations, where people from hamlets and outlying farms gathered to share a meal and drink the local wine. Today, when television, the Internet, cell phones, cars, and swimming pools are the norm, *la fête campagnarde* lives on in the village feasts where locals, visitors, and tourists sit down together at long tables in the village square for *le grand aïoli.*

In many of the villages of Provence, the feast is held on August 15. Initially, it seemed strange to me that so many villages decided to have community feasts at the same time, until I learned that August 15 is the date of the Catholic Feast of the Assumption, celebrating the assumption, body and soul, of the Virgin Mary into heaven. The religious import of the feast is still recognized with special masses and pilgrimages, but the secular aspect seems to take precedence. The festivities go on at least for two days, beginning on August 14. They generally include *boules* matches during the day, live music, *apéritifs* and dancing from seven to eight in the evening, and a *grand bal* with more live music and dancing into the night. On August 15, there is an *apèritif* at noon, followed by *le grand aïoli* and more *boules* matches. In late July, posters tacked on telephone poles and taped onto the windows of *cafés* and *boulangeries* announce the upcoming feast, the schedule of activities, the cost of the meal, and where to buy the tickets, plus a reminder to bring your own tableware.

....

The first time I went to *le grand aïoli* in my village, Donald, Ethel, Oliver, and I arrived a little early, not knowing quite what to expect. Even though it wasn't quite noon, a lot of people had already staked out their places. We found space for the four of us between a young German-speaking couple and a group of French people, probably a family with friends and relatives. Ethel spotted Aileen, Marie and Marcel's daughter, and ran off to meet her, her pink sundress flying behind her and her white leather sandals flinging dust. Oliver followed, smartly dressed in what he called his party clothes, creamy muslin pull-on pants and a matching T-shirt trimmed with red, yellow, and green braid.

I waved to Aileen and then set out our dishes, flea market finds with an art deco–style border in black and dark green, green cloth napkins, and stainless-steel knives and forks that I had brought from California. We used the same short bistro-style glasses for wine that most everyone else did. Donald went to the *apéritif* bar set up under the trees in front of the *mairie*, city hall, at the far end of the square. As soon as I finished, I put my basket under the table and joined him. We saw a few people we had a nodding acquaintance with, and they asked about Oliver and Ethel. We pointed them out, playing across the way, and noted that the children were very happy to be back in Provence. When

Oliver was born, he had been the first baby born in the village in more than ten years, and the small community considered him to be special, and people had always liked the little American girl who had come to live in their midst.

Donald and I both had a *pastis* and nibbled on olives and potato chips as we looked around. The square was filling slowly with whirling colors as people, dressed in summer brights, moved around the tables talking, their dishes and glasses rattling in the background as they emptied their baskets and set their places. Men put bottles of wine on the tables, unlabeled and corks removed, and then set out more wine bottles filled with water instead of wine. A microphone stood alone on the bandstand, where the band had played the previous night, and the mayor was starting up the stairs to the stand. He was a local farmer, heavy and with big powerful arms and hands, and very taciturn whenever I had occasion to meet him. He was one of the many mayors in the *département* of the Var at that time who were communists, and it was rumored that he had been a leader in the local *Résistance.* One never knows. I had always been somewhat in awe of him, so it was strange to watch him laugh, smile, and call out and wave to friends, telling everyone *"À table, à table!"* before he gave a very brief welcome to the crowd and went back to sit down with his family. A tape recorder began to play music that sounded to me like accordion polkas.

I poured water for Ethel and Oliver, and Donald poured us *rosé,* then passed the bottle down the table. I had expected the food to be out when we sat down, but only baskets of bread were on the table. The French family next to us seemed calm, chatting away, so I assumed all was well and that the food would arrive in due course. Not long after, I saw Marie heading our way carrying a cardboard flat, the kind that vegetables are packed in.

She paused at the end of our table, took something out of the box, and put it on a plate. She repeated this, and by the time she neared us, I saw she was placing handfuls of cooked green beans on everyone's plates. She looked festive, her hair recently done (I had seen her friend, a traveling *coiffeuse*, hairdresser, come to her house the day before), and was wearing a bright red blouse, a flowered print skirt, and red wedge sandals.

171

"*Et pour toi, Georgeanne, et toi Ethel, et toi Oliver, et toi Donald.*" She put a healthy handful of beans on each of our plates. "More is coming!" She moved on, and then I saw women with cardboard boxes, laughing, their hands reaching in and out of the boxes they carried. Soon our plates had boiled potatoes, beets, and carrots, as well as beans, hard-cooked eggs, and snails.

Snails were not new to us—we had hunted them the previous summer—and we were delighted to see them on the table. We had gathered a goodly amount of snails at Sillans-la-Cascade, plucking them from the slippery rocks where they had ventured out from the ivy-covered walls after the rain.

After we fed the snails thyme and bran for two weeks, Marie helped us cook them. We then took them out of their shells, cut off the bitter tips, and stuffed them back into their shells. We made a tomato sauce heavily seasoned with garlic and put the stuffed shells in the sauce to simmer for more than two hours. Finally, according to Marie's instructions, we ate them *à la sucarelle*, with our fingers, sucking the snails from their shells, with a little help from toothpicks. Messy, but good.

....

Snails have been eaten in Provence since the earliest times, not in sauces but cooked in or over coals. Remains of ashes and snail shells have been found in the entrances of prehistoric caves in the region of Haute-Provence, some dating to at least 11,000 B.C.E. Archaeologists have even unearthed several sites where such an impressive number of snail shells have been found that the sites are sometimes referred to as Mesolithic *escargotières,* or snail farms. Even in Quinson, not far from our house, there is evidence that prehistoric humans ate snails, and I like to think that the snails we gathered were descendants from those prehistoric times.

The people of Provence continue the tradition of cooking snails in coals, and locals have told me that until the 1950s and 1960s, it was common to cook snails for lunch while working in the vineyards. The workers would build a fire of grape prunings in a clearing and place a rack over the coals to hold the snails, just the way their grandparents and great-grandparents did. The snails were picked from their shells with a pin or a needle and ideally would have been eaten with lots of *aïoli.* In Marseille in the 1930s, snail vendors plied their wares in the streets, selling paper cones of snails accompanied by a pick. During the early part of the twentieth century, eating snails *à la sucarelle,* as we had, was one of the family feasts of preference.

········

Moments after the vegetables and snails were delivered to our table, more women, this time came carrying big bowls, appeared, stopping at every place. When two arrived at our side, they asked, "*Aïoli* made with olive oil or sunflower oil? The one with sunflower oil is *moins fort,* not as strong." I always made my *aïoli* with olive oil, so I chose that, but decided to take the *moins fort* for Oliver. He might prefer a milder version, and that way I could taste it too.

One woman stepped up and put a heaping ladleful on my plate, Donald's, and Ethel's, while the other woman gave a ladleful to Oliver. This *aïoli* was pale yellow, not greenish gold like the olive oil version I had chosen. I sampled it, dipping a piece of bread into it. It was almost buttery tasting, but very garlicky. I tried mine. Very garlicky too, but stronger, fruitier, with the hint of the bitter aftertaste characteristic of olive oil. I liked them both. I later learned that unless the olive oil is a mild, Provençal-style oil, like the one I used, it is a good idea to make *aïoli* with a combination of olive oil and grapeseed or sunflower oil, unless you love the deep bite and sometimes fiery, bitter finish of a strong olive oil.

173

The differences in taste among extra-virgin olive oils, the type I use, whether for cooking or making vinaigrette, or as a condiment, can be substantial. Variables include the variety of olive, or olives if a blend; the location of the grove; and the growing, harvesting, and milling conditions. A major factor determining taste is the maturity of the olives when picked. Olives harvested when still partially green will produce an oil that has a bitter or hot aftertaste, while an oil made with fully mature, black olives will be mild and fruity, almost buttery. The difference is similar to that between a green bell pepper, which is picked immature, and a mature red one. Most Provençal olive oils fall somewhere in between. Traditionally, the olives in Provence are harvested when they are black, or nearly so, and consequently the Provençal oils are milder than those of Tuscany, for example, where the olives are picked when still partially green.

Classic Provençal preparations other than *aïoli* rely on the partnership of garlic and olive oil. *Tapenade*, a tangy olive paste spread on toasts or vegetables, begins, like *aïoli*, with crushing garlic and salt together. Olives and capers are added, and sometimes herbs or nuts, then the olive oil is slowly drizzled in until the paste is the desired consistency. *Anchoïade* begins the same way, but instead of olives, anchovies are added before the olive oil is drizzled in.

"Oliver, let me taste your *aïoli*. This one is too hot and I don't like it." Ethel reached toward the gleaming pale yellow mound on his plate. He was sticking to the eggs, potatoes, and bread. After one taste of the *aïoli* at my encouragement, he decided not to eat more.

174   "Take it. I don't want it."

Ethel took a big spoonful for her plate, pushing aside her *aïoli*. "Mmm. I like this one better," she said.

When the women with the bowls and cardboard boxes circled back, Ethel's *aïoli* was almost gone, as was mine and Donald's. This time there was something new— pieces of *morue*, salt cod.

I had eaten salt cod only once, on New Year's Eve when Oliver was two months old. Georgette and Denys, our neighbors, had invited us to a midnight supper, and the first course was a salt cod and leek *gratin,* Denys's favorite dish. It was unforgettable. The top was crispy with golden bread crumbs. Beneath them were tiny flakes of the cured fish and sweet leeks bound together with a creamy *béchamel* sauce just slightly piquant with cayenne. I had never prepared salt cod, nor had I eaten it in a chunk like the one I had just been served. I watched the people around me remove the silver-gray skin and pick off any fins or pieces of bone or cartilage before separating the fish into large flakes and dipping them into or spreading them with *aïoli*. I did the same. The texture of the fish was coarse and somewhat grainy, the flavor strong but good, especially with the *aïoli*. I liked it, and that summer I determined I'd find out how to prepare salt cod.

It wasn't difficult. The first step is to soak the cod for twenty-four hours in several changes of water, which not only rehydrates the fish but leaches out the salt. Once that's accomplished, the fish is poached along with a bay leaf. I always cut off a small piece of the fish first, poach it, then taste it to make sure that all but a hint of the salt is gone. If not, I rinse the fish under cold running water, poach another piece, and taste again before poaching the whole fish.

The poached fish is ready to eat, in pieces with *aïoli,* or used in preparations like leek and salt cod *gratin* or *brandade de morue,* one of the great dishes of Provence. True *brandade* is nothing more than poached salt cod, hot olive oil, and hot milk, beaten on the stove top over gentle heat until a thick, creamy emulsion forms. As with so many very simple things, it is not as easy as it sounds. The oil must not be added too quickly, nor can it be too hot or it will not emulsify. The milk must be handled with care. It should be added slowly and not be too hot, lest it curdle and ruin the *brandade,* which, above all, must never be allowed to boil. Once the emulsion is successfully formed, a *persillade,* a mixture of crushed garlic cloves, parsley, and lemon, is added. Served with *croûtons* and red wine, it is a queenly dish made from humble ingredients.

A simpler, less challenging version of *brandade* uses potatoes. It is simpler because it is not an emulsion, and is also milder and less intense than the purist version. To make it, the poached fish is crushed with a mortar and pestle or puréed, then is mashed with potatoes. Alternating streams of hot milk and olive oil are beaten in to form a thick, creamy paste, the *persillade* is added, and the mixture is spread into a *gratin* dish, topped with bread crumbs, and drizzled with olive oil before being baked in a hot oven. It, too, is served with *croûtons.*

Until relatively recently, salt cod was considered poor people's food. An old Provençal saying used to praise an exotic or deluxe dish loosely translates as "It's sure not salt cod and spinach," a combination that, so I have heard, was common family fare in households with economic restraints. Today, salt cod costs as much per kilo as beefsteak or fresh tuna, and former peasant dishes like *brandade de morue* are served in fine restaurants. The *brandade* might be offered as an *amuse-bouche* on a bite-size toast with a sliver of black truffle or in combination with fresh poached cod alongside a black olive *tapenade.*

··················

176

We finished our first *grand aïoli* that day with pastries from the local bakery. The baker and his wife, bound in white aprons, and their helpers passed among the tables with glossy white bakery boxes full of exquisite *petits fours*, small tarts filled with chocolate *mousse* or fresh fruit, delicate *mille-feuilles*, and bite-size almond *meringues*. They gave Oliver and Ethel two each, which my children promptly finished before going to play with Aileen, who was jumping rope in the distance. Donald and I settled back to have one more glass of wine and watch the changing scene, as people began drifting away from the tables to the *boules* match, leaving their picnic baskets behind.

Boules, properly called *pétanque*, is the ultimate sport in Provence. Everyone plays it—young and old, men and women. A *boules* match is easy to spot. Five or more people looking down at packed dirt or sand, usually in a shady spot, indicate that a match is under way. On closer inspection you'll see that they are staring at steel balls—the *boules*—trying to determine which one is closest to a small wooden ball, the *cochonnet* or *coche*. The object of the game, which is similar to lawn bowling and *bocce*, is to plant your feet close together and throw the *boules* as close as possible to the *coche*, placed six to ten meters away. The game is played between teams of one, two, or three people, with each team having six balls. When all the balls have been thrown, very careful measuring takes place with a folding steel tape that most players keep in their pockets or with calipers if the distances are short. The winning team gets one point for every ball that is closer to the *coche* than any of the opponents' balls. Play continues to thirteen points.

Watching *boules* matches is a serious spectator sport in Provence, and crowds stand around, eyes shifting from *boule* to *coche* to players and back with every toss. Donald and I joined the spectators after we finished our wine and packed up our dishes. One of our friends was playing, and he had been nervous about the competition he might draw, since top players often come from neighboring villages to compete in the August 15 matches, where prizes are awarded.

The crowd was large, and many of the men were drinking *pastis*. We stood on the edge, close enough to see players give a good-luck pull to their cap's bill, bend over and pick up a little dirt, and rub it between their hands to ensure a good grip on the *boule*. Everyone looked serious as a competitor stepped up to the line drawn in the earth and aimed a shot. We stayed long enough to watch the mixed teams—two men and one woman per team—play matches. The women were just as earnest and, in some cases, just as good or even better than the men, but their attire was more varied. One woman, very tan and sleek with blonde hair perfectly cut to shoulder length, wore a thin-strapped white cotton sundress that ended well above her shapely knees. A lot of the men in the crowd shifted behind her to watch her throw. Another woman, stern faced with a work-lined visage, her brown hair in a tight perm, wore serviceable brown shoes and a green-and-blue plaid skirt well below her knees. She drew the men's attention not for her shape and attire, but for her unerring aim as she repeatedly knocked an opponent's ball away from the *coche*.

By four o'clock, Ethel and Oliver were getting hot and bored and wanted to go swimming in the lake. I was hot, too, and a swim sounded like a good way to end the day.

Le Grand Aïoli

AN AÏOLI FEAST

At the heart of the feast is the greenish gold, garlicky mayonnaise. The simplest and, I think, best way to prepare the feast at home is to follow the example of Provençal villages and serve the aïoli with boiled or steamed vegetables, hard-cooked eggs, and fish.

Start the event with a few appetizers and glasses of *pastis* or *rosé*, then bring out the vegetables, followed by the fish, all accompanied by plenty of sliced *baguettes* and wine. Finish the meal with fruit tarts, and you have a Provençal feast right in your own backyard.

To make the *aïoli*, using a pestle, crush four cloves of garlic in a mortar with a pinch of coarse sea salt until you get a paste. If you have a large mortar, continue using it. If not, remove the crushed garlic to a bowl. Whisk in three large egg yolks. Drop by drop, drizzle in about ½ cup extra-virgin olive oil, whisking continuously. As the *aïoli* begins to thicken, the oil can be added in a thin, steady stream. If you are using a mild Provençal-style olive oil, continue whisking in another ½ cup olive oil. If the olive oil is strong, whisk in ½ cup grapeseed or sunflower oil instead. In either case, whisk just until the *aïoli* is stiff. Set aside. The *aïoli* can be made a day ahead, but becomes stronger over time.

For eight people, I typically boil twelve eggs, sixteen to twenty small gold or red beets, sixteen to twenty small fingerling or other boiling potatoes, eight or ten carrots, cut in half, and 2 pounds green beans. You can adjust the quantities according to your and your guests' personal tastes and appetites.

For the fish, I like to poach salmon fillets and serve them at room temperature. For eight people, I use eight salmon fillets, each about ⅓ pound. I poach them in a large frying pan half filled with water, to which I add a ½ cup dry white wine, 1 tablespoon coarse sea salt, the juice of one lemon, and a few sprigs of fresh tarragon. I simmer this mixture, covered, for 10 minutes, then add the fillets, and cook, spooning them with liquid, until they are just opaque and easily flake with a fork. I remove the fillets to a platter and cover them loosely with foil until serving. The salmon can be cooked in the morning and refrigerated, then brought to room temperature.

To serve, bring platters and bowls of eggs and vegetables to the table, accompanied by the *aïoli* and bread. Shortly thereafter, serve the fish.

SERVES 8

CHAPTER 7

SHEEP AND
PIEDS-ET-PAQUETS

Traditions of the transhumance. *No part of the lamb goes to waste.
A butcher at work. A* méchoui *from the Ivory Coast.*

We had to stop the car. We were surrounded by sheep, and the
narrow mountain road with its precipitous drop didn't encourage cavalier attitudes about whether man or beast ruled. We
rolled down the windows and waited, caught in a sea of moving
animals and unfamiliar sounds as their clanging bells competed
with their bleating and the sharp piercing whistles of the shepherds. Elegant, stately goats, mixed in the flocks, gracefully
sprang over the backs of the trudging sheep to land on nearby
rocks or scaled the cliffs on the far side of the road to eat an
especially tasty branch or morsel of grass before being nipped
down by the grayish black sheepdogs. The sheep, keeping their
long, smooth faces slightly bent toward the ground, steadily
moved forward and past us, pushed on by the determined
pressure of the shepherds and the dogs.

As the animals brushed against the sides of the car, we could smell their wettish wool, permeated with the strong resinous scent of the scrubby forest they had just passed through. We could see the bits of juniper and pine needles clinging to their matted coats.

The shepherds that day were a mixed bunch, some in full-blown Provençal shepherd regalia with broad-brimmed flat-crowned black felt hats, sweeping brown or black coats with capes, and strong well-worn shepherd's crooks. Others wore heavy wool *bérets* pulled down over their eyes and knobby, thick sweaters, hand knitted, I suspected, of wool from a previous season's shearing.

"Is this the *transhumance*?" I asked the man tending the small *café* where we stopped for sandwiches just short of our destination, the Col d'Allos, as we watched the streets of the village fill with the sheep, goats, dogs, and shepherds we had passed through earlier. The shepherds were working hard to keep the animals away from the trees lining the road and the flowering plants in the small park across from the restaurant, snapping whips over the sheep's heads and calling at the dogs that ran alongside. I could see the sweat dripping down the face of the shepherd closest to us as he hurried by, completely focused on the animals in his charge. The proprietor turned back from the doorway where we all stood watching, and as the last of them passed through the street, he answered me.

"Yes. They come through here every June 25 or so. We're the second to last village before they climb up into the high pastures. They're coming from around St-Rémy, and it takes them ten days to get here, and then one more day to the pastures. They're going to stop just on the other side of the village and camp until around one o'clock in the morning. Let everyone sleep. Animals too. It's too hot to walk in the afternoon."

We sat down and he brought the drinks we ordered, cold, clean draft beer for me and Donald, Oranginas for Ethel and Oliver. He reappeared shortly with a plate stacked with four *baguette* sandwiches of ham and butter, each wrapped with a small square of parchment paper. Almost nothing tastes as good for lunch as a French-style ham sandwich with a cold beer. The bread, at least one-third of a crusty *baguette* from a late-morning bake, is cut lengthwise and heavily slathered with sweet butter before two or three slices of thin ham are folded in half down the center and the sandwich closed up. That's it. Three tastes, three textures.

We were hungry after our long drive and all the excitement, so we ate quietly for a few minutes, savoring each bite before we started talking about what we had seen. We had caught glimpses of sheep before, in the distance, and heard their bells, but this was the first time we had been amid the moving flock. It would happen again over subsequent summers, and also during the fall, when the sheep are brought down from the high pastures to spend the winter in the low country.

Sheep have been an important economic resource in Provence since Roman times, and the *transhumance* has been practiced since "the night of time," as shepherds like to say. No evidence exists for the prehistoric period, but in early Roman writings there are references to the *drailles*, or trails, followed by the sheep. Sheep, like goats, are suited to the hardscrabble life of the dry Mediterranean ecosystem and have adapted to eating its sparse grasses and herbs. When the weather becomes torrid, as it does in the summer months, they don't eat and consequently they lose weight and their health can suffer.

Although the departure dates vary, the great *troupeaux* from southwestern Provence in the region around St-Rémy and Arles, each numbering in the thousands, set out around the tenth of June

183

and head northeast to the Valley of Ubraye, to the Piémont and the mountains of the Alpes-Maritimes, crossing the Col d'Allos. The *troupeaux* from the southeastern part of Provence, around Manosque and Aups, where the temperature stays cooler longer, leave for the high pastures around the fifteenth of June. The trek takes ten to twelve days, and the animals and their human companions walk about fifteen kilometers a day, starting well after midnight, when it's cool, and stopping in late morning when the sun begins to beat down. Part of the traveling occurs along roads, like the one we were on near the Col d'Allos, but much is done along dirt tracks, the *drailles*, that cross the countryside, cutting through forests, along the edges of cultivated fields, and through the scrubby *garrigue*. Trucks carrying the food, cooking gear, grain, and medicine travel with each *troupeau*, ready to pick up any unfit traveler, beast or human, and to set up the daily camp. There was a time during the 1970s when it looked like the tradition of the *transhumance* on foot might die out, superseded by diesel trucks filled with the bleating animals that could make the journey from the sun-parched south to the mountain pastures in a day. But due to the stress of the travel by truck, the sheep lost weight and some even died, so the older, kinder—and more practical—movement of animals resumed, much to the delight of the villages along the way whose residents counted on seeing the sheep and shepherds at the same time every year.

Although thousands of sheep are still trucked, the threat to the traditional *transhumance* seems to have dissipated. Young entrepreneurial sheepherders, both men and women, are taking professional training to prepare themselves for what used to be only a hands-on learning experience. Part of the training is in the classroom and barns; the remainder is on the road, as apprentices in the *transhumance* with a master shepherd.

184

After a brief training session, friends and interested parties can participate in the *transhumance*, something that I have always wanted to do.

My friend Joanne went once and declared it to be a transcendental experience. "There is nothing comparable to being out on those high plateaus with only you and the stars, surrounded by the warmth of over a thousand animals. Their smell becomes part of your world, and you learn to distinguish the differences in their sounds, even to tell them apart. There were ten of us, and each of us was responsible for one hundred sheep throughout the trip, making sure they didn't eat the geraniums in the villages, fall off a cliff, or run in front of a car."

I asked about the rain, and Joanne said it didn't really matter. It wasn't cold except on the highest passes, and everyone dried out while they walked, as the sheep did. A few people, she told me, had bloodied feet after the first few days and had to drop out.

"Everyone helped cook when we stopped. The truck carried tables and benches and basic food. One night a deer wandered into the camp, and a shepherd shot it. We had it for dinner the next night, but I couldn't eat it. It was tough and tasted like the smell of blood."

In the days before supply trucks, much of the food was supplied by hunting, whether it was humble fare like squirrels and marmots or the deer and mountain sheep that inhabit the higher elevations, or the unlucky sheep or lamb that was mortally injured on the trek.

······················

Since sheep have been such an integral part of their lives for centuries, supplying not only meat but wool and skins for clothing and tallow for candles, it's not surprising that the Provençaux have devised ways to eat every part of the animal. *Les abats*, the offal, are still considered among the most desirable parts of the animal, and great attention is given to preparing the kidneys, heart, and even the tongue. Lamb's tongue salad is a *bistro* favorite throughout France. The tongue, small and delicate, is poached in broth, seasoned, sliced, and then tossed with olive oil, parsley, and minced garlic. Less likely to be found, if at all, are two preparations, one for the stomach lining and feet, the other for the feet alone. Both are distinctly Provençal and speak eloquently about the culinary passion of the Provençaux and the importance of sheep.

Pieds-et-paquets, literally "feet" (or lamb trotters) "and packets," are a Marseille specialty that rivals *bouillabaisse* as the culinary signature of the city, although Sisteron lays claim to them as well.

The packets are made by stuffing squares of stomach lining, also called tripe, with minced garlic, parsley, and bacon, then folding the squares into packets. These are cooked for about five hours in a sauce of tomato, white wine, and aromatics, along with the trotters and a thick slice of pork belly. No thickening agent is added because the sauce is naturally thickened by the gelatin in the feet. It is a rich and rustic dish, one that I love for its complex flavor, delicate yet slightly chewy texture, and orange-red sauce. Not everyone relishes the idea of eating such strange fare, but the dish holds an iconic place in the familial memory of Provence, and I know many people who rapturously tuck into a plate of *paquets* swimming in the thick sauce, and even pick the scant meat from the feet.

By the time the packets have cooked in their fragrant sauce, the tripe has become mild and so tender that the thin, meaty bits melt with the first bite, releasing the garlic and parsley stuffing to blend with a little of the sauce. Sometimes minced tripe is added to the stuffing, making for a slightly more intense, but no less succulent, eating experience.

The last artisanal *pieds-et-paquets* factory in Haute-Provence is in Sisteron, the gateway to Provence. Sisteron, located at the crossroads of the Alpine and lowland regions of Provence, and thus at the crossroads of the *transhumance*, has several large slaughterhouses and is well known for its *pieds-et-paquets*. If I see ready-made *pieds-et-paquets* for sale at butcher shops in Sisteron or elsewhere in the upper region, from Manosque to Forcalquier, I buy them. They are easy to spot. The feet, ivory white and very smooth, are stacked neatly on stainless-steel or white-enameled trays, with the tripe-wrapped packets next to them, usually garnished with sprigs of parsley. I have never made my own *paquets* from start to finish, though I'd like to. However, I've never been disappointed by the ones I've purchased. Whether making homemade or ready-made *pieds-et-paquets*, the sauce is the same. Canned tomatoes and their juice, white wine, pork belly, bay leaf, thyme, salt, and pepper are brought to a simmer and the *paquets* are added. The pot is covered and the sauce is simmered for two hours. The feet are added, and after another two or three hours of slow simmering, the tripe is tender and the dish is ready to serve.

This is just one example of the lengths that Provençal cooks, often of modest means living in isolated farmhouses, have gone to in order to prepare not just good food, but food that lives on in memory, refueling the spirit each time it is eaten. In listening to people recount their food memories around a table, I've seen their eyes glow and their body language soften with the telling of the taste, smell, and texture of a beloved dish, and heard the smack of lips in reply.

One memorable instance involves another lamb's foot preparation, *beignets des pieds d'agneaux,* or lamb's foot fritters.

187

I remember Marie's cousin Josephine talking with Marcel's aunt, who, at ninety, was a hearty eater and enjoyed her wine. She was as fine a listener as a raconteur.

As we sat under the mulberry trees on the terrace at Robert and Françoise Lamy's house, just across the road from mine, finishing the celebratory lunch that ended the grape harvest, Marie's cousin asked *la tante,* a tiny woman with a wrinkled birdlike face, if she remembered when they used to make lamb's feet *beignets.* I listened raptly as they recounted memories of long ago.

"Oh my, do I. So much work. First scraping them, then flaming them to burn off any wool left, like burning feathers off a chicken. Then we blanched them to get them nice and white. We'd have a pot of at least twelve, sometimes more, going on the *braise.* No one cooks on a *braise* anymore." She laughed and shook her head, her thin gray hair catching on the breeze.

"Oh my, but they were good. Once they were cooked, we'd sit around, my daughters, my mother, my grandmother, children, all of us around the big wooden table, gossiping and telling stories, sometimes with a glass of *eau-de-vie* to keep us warm. I'd cut each foot in half, hitting it hard with a cleaver, then hand them out. We picked out the bones, then picked out the meat. The skins were set aside to be stuffed. All the meat came back to me and I chopped it very fine with the wild thyme. Next I added the salt and pepper, sometimes anchovies, if we had them, and mixed it all with olive oil. Everyone took a little stuffing and stuffed the skin of the half foot, then we put them back together, binding them with string. Whew. What work in the old days!"

"Ah, that's how you did it," Josephine said. "I just remember the taste and being astonished that it looked like a foot, but had no bones. What next?"

"Next? Ah, ah, yes." She paused, then pulled the train of thought back to herself.

"Yes, next, well, we dipped them in flour or bread crumbs and fried them in a deep pot of olive oil."

"We ate them with lemons, didn't we? And a sprinkle of parsley, too, I think. I loved the way they were crunchy on the outside, soft and meaty on the inside. I remember stealing them off Raymond's plate." Josephine said, looking down the table at her brother.

189

"You were a bad sister. You took them when you knew I wasn't looking, then lied about it. But Tatie always gave me more anyway." He laughed and poured himself a little more wine.

"Could we make some?" I asked Josephine and Marie, fascinated by the idea and imagining how good they must taste. "*Ah, non*. It's too much work," they both replied, letting the memory be enough for them.

Nevertheless I was determined to make them, but it wasn't until recently that I did. The feet took more than two hours to cook, and I tore some of the skin when picking out the bones, which wasn't catastrophic, but the stuffing poked out. The feet looked a little lumpy after I bound the two sides together, but they were recognizable. I learned that the dish was basically a type of terrine. You can accomplish a similar dish by wrapping the meat mixture in plastic wrap and poaching it for about ten minutes. After the packets are chilled, the meat is sliced, breaded, and fried. The combination of the crunchy texture, aromatic herbs, and delicate meat is held together by the gelatin and sinews that dissolve during the initial cooking. Just like *pieds-et-paquets*, lamb's foot fritters make for an eating experience that is well worth the effort.

....

Any dish is only as good as the ingredients you begin with, and in Provence the finest lamb is considered to be Sisteron lamb, characteristically sweet, mild meat from lambs that graze on the wild herbs and grasses of Haute-Provence and are slaughtered locally. This regional specialty has been awarded an Indication Géographique Protégée, an official EU designation that merits the Red Label, which guarantees to consumers a top-quality European product.

In this case, the label ensures that the animal was born, raised, and slaughtered in the area of production under certain established rules and conditions. For example, the reproductive herd of ewes and rams must be composed of three regional breeds: Mérinos d'Arles, Préalpes du Sud, or Mourerous, or crosses of these breeds. The herds must also practice the traditional grazing patterns inherent in the *transhumance*, the lambs must be raised on their mothers' milk for a minimum of sixty days, and the lambs must have traceability at all stages, from reproduction to slaughter and transport. A lamb must weigh between twelve and nineteen kilos and be between seventy and one hundred fifty days old at the time of slaughter.

A butcher shop, such as the one I go to in Aups, that sells Sisteron lamb proudly advertises so with a sticker in the shop window bearing a drawing of a fluffy lamb and "Agneau de Sisteron" printed on it. The meat of a Sisteron lamb is firm yet tender, and as my butcher tells me, a *gigot* is perfectly cooked after only forty-five minutes at the equivalent of 375 degrees Fahrenheit. I've found that shopkeepers and vendors are more than happy to tell you the different ways to cook or prepare what you are buying from them.

"Now," the butcher says to me each time I buy a leg of lamb, "you be sure to rub it all over with olive oil, then lots of fresh

thyme, a little fresh rosemary, then make slits about this deep"—
he indicates them with his thumb and forefinger—"and fill them
all with garlic slivers. Don't overcook it. Nothing worse than a
nice *gigot* spoiled by overcooking."

He and his wife look alike, both *costaud*, or hefty, with round
faces and big wide smiles, though his hair is white, matching his
apron, and hers a soft brown.

"Ah," his wife often says, as she adds a gift, a house-made
saucisson pour l'apéritif, to my purchases, "you are so lucky to
have a nice *gigot*. I love them, but no one else in my family does,
and my husband, poor soul, can't eat them anymore. No point
my cooking a *gigot* just for myself."

I like to peek through the shop door into the back. The
butcher disappears behind the heavy door of his cold room, then
emerges with a whole lamb or a quarter of a hog carcass slung
over his shoulder, drops it onto to his thick, scarred butcher
block, pulls one of his long knives from the rack behind the
block, and sharpens it with fluid arcs against the steel. Soon I
can't see his movements because his back is to the shop front, his
head bent over his work. Shortly he reappears with a pork loin
or a neatly tied roast larded with thin slices of back fat, a sprig
of thyme held beneath the string, or a rack of lamb loin chops,
perfectly trimmed.

Once, I asked him about *rognonnade*, a cut I had seen in the
window of a butcher shop in another town a couple of hours
away, but I was on a summer day's excursion and couldn't buy it
for fear that it would spoil.

"Ah, now that is a noble cut. Did you see it whole or was it
sliced into chops?"

"Sliced. There were four pieces that looked like . . .," I
searched for a word, "well, like eyeglasses." I cupped my hands,

nearly touching the fingertips to show him. "They were two centimeters or so thick"—I demonstrated the thickness with a thumb and forefinger—"and each of the two sides were wrapped around a bit of kidney."

"Yes, cut from the *selle,* the lower part of the back." He turned, putting his hands on his lower back to show me. "Right here, where the kidneys are." Turning back to me, he said, "So when you cut those chops, you can cut each with a slice of kidney. It's a delicate matter to do, one for a real butcher, not those people behind the counter in *grande surface* where all they do is arrange precut meat on trays. Those supermarket butchers, they don't butcher the carcasses themselves. That takes knowledge and expertise."

I had heard similar opinions from him and other butchers about the current state of the *métier,* the demise of the true butcher, and the lack of young people to come behind him and his generation when they retire.

"Now, the *selle* can also be cooked whole, but I haven't filled an order for that in quite a while. I don't know if anyone knows how to cook it anymore. It used to be I sold several every holiday season, which isn't bad for a village of fifteen hundred people."

I was intrigued by all this and immediately ordered a *rognonnade* chop. He went into the cooler in the back of the shop and came out with the hindquarters of a lamb on his shoulder, flipped it down on his butcher block, wielded his knives, and brought me a chop for my inspection. It looked just like the one I had seen earlier and I could hardly wait to cook it.

That night I rubbed the chop with olive oil, fresh thyme, and sea salt. I crushed some black peppercorns in a mortar and rubbed that over it as well. Since it was early September, and still warm, I didn't want to grill the meat in the fireplace as I would have later in the season, and instead broiled it, for just four or five minutes per side. "You don't want to cook it too long," the butcher had told me, "or you'll ruin the kidneys. They get tough when they're overcooked."

The kidneys, two small, rosy bites, were cooked to perfection, as was the rest of the chop. I ate it with creamed spinach, one of my favorite dishes, and slices of fresh tomato from the garden, and poured some Gigondas.

If *selles*, or "barons" in English, and *gigots* are the noble cuts, the other cuts aspire to the same heights, though they require, like the feet, more time and inventiveness. In the traditional rural households where home butchery was routine—this lasted well into the 1970s and even longer in the remote regions in the mountains—several lambs would be fattened and slaughtered over the course of a year. Any injured lamb or sheep was slaughtered as well, and consequently there was a substantial supply of meat, none of it to be wasted.

Old people tell of preparing the inelegant parts of the animals, like the trotters, heads, testicles, kidneys, heart, blood, and breasts. Some of these, like the *pieds-et-paquets, brochettes de rognons, blanquette d'agneau*, and *soupe courte*, can still be found in homes and family restaurants across Provence, classics handed down through generations. Since goats were kept as well, the preparations were used interchangeably for *chevreaux*.

Brochettes, for example, made with pieces of lamb's kidney, heart, and liver interspersed with onion, green peppers, and bacon, all well seasoned, are omnipresent at festivals, grilled alongside sausages by sidewalk vendors and sold by the skewer. The vendor also gives you a chunk of *baguette* slit open. You put the skewer inside, clamp down on the bread, and pull the skewer, removing it. You'll also find ready-to-cook skewers, packed in Styrofoam trays and covered with plastic wrap, in any supermarket.

Soupe courte, short soup, is made from the lesser cuts of lamb such as the neck and the breast, though sometimes chops are used. The meat is browned in rendered lard or olive oil along with onions, garlic, carrots, and herbs, then very slowly simmered in a little broth. Once it is done, which takes about two hours, water is poured in the pot and brought to a boil, and rice, saffron, and more seasonings are added. The soup, called "short" because there is not a lot of it, resembles a thick rice porridge. It is served in a bowl, with the meat alongside, which can then be removed from the bones and stirred into the soup. This substantial soup is a favorite on the menus of traditional family-style restaurants and *bistros* throughout Provence, a sign that people still revere and enjoy the old preparations, and seek to preserve them.

Lamb or mutton breasts are held together with muscle and cartilage and are small, not very meaty, and often quite fatty. The ingenious Provençaux cook them like *blanquette de veau*, the classic French veal breast stew, giving them a long simmer in a broth aromatic with a *bouquet garni*, onions, and carrots, skimming and straining the liquid and finally finishing with a creamy, white, egg-based sauce to create a *plat* worthy of any good *bourgeois* household.

Lamb breasts are an inexpensive cut of meat, even today, and like other inexpensive cuts, they take time and care to prepare successfully. I've stuffed them, according to directions from my neighbor Marie, as I would a boneless breast of veal, with a mix of ham, *lardons*, mushrooms, and shallots, adding some spices. I braised the stuffed breast, resting on its bones in broth, for an hour or more. I let it cool just a bit to let the juices jell, then cut the meat into slices, which makes a presentation as elegant as the dish tastes. I've even barbecued lamb ribs, marinating them first in a classic American-style barbecue sauce. This was my own idea, but not a success. They were not meaty enough to eat like pork or beef ribs, in spite of the spicy sauce, and tasted fatty.

Truly frugal Provençal housewives, those who lived through the war years, would remove the heavy skin covering the breast, stitch the sides together to make a pocket, and fill it with a savory stuffing of bread, herbs, maybe a little sausage, all held together with olive oil, then bake the pocket. Allowed to chill, it was cut into thin slices and served for a first course, with or without mustard or some other piquant sauce. The breast was cooked separately in a stew or other preparation. Removing the skin and stuffing it allowed the cook to make two dishes from a very modest cut of meat.

195

....

When Donald and I returned to California, I longed for the foods that we had in Provence, so we bought and slaughtered the occasional pig and found lamb to buy on the hoof.

At the high school where Donald taught agriculture and animal husbandry, there was an active FFA club, Future Farmers of America, for which the teachers were responsible. One of the members worked weekends at the Dixon Livestock Auction, the area's last auction yard, and when I met him at an FFA party, he told me he could buy lamb there for about sixty dollars, a price that would include cutting it up. That sounded wonderful to me, and Donald and I arranged to buy a lamb through him. When we received it, it was neatly packaged and labeled as chops, leg, shoulder, ribs, and stew, plus one package labeled liver, kidney, and heart, much to my delight.

When I grilled the first chops, though, I learned that this was definitely what we call mutton, an older animal with a strong taste, not like the lamb we had eaten in Provence. A veterinarian friend, who also raised lambs and had lamb cookouts every spring on his ranch, explained that the strong taste was in the fat and advised me to trim off as much as possible before cooking the lamb, which I then started to do.

The meat was rich and flavorful, and I came to like the strong background taste. I felt linked to my Provençal life by cooking it, even though the taste was different.

....

Provence, like other parts of Europe and North Africa bordering on the Mediterranean, has been exposed to other cultures over the centuries through invasion, conquest, and immigration, and this is apparent in the food. Algerian independence in 1961 brought a new wave of immigrants to Provence, followed by immigrants from the former French colonies of Morocco, Senegal, and the Ivory Coast, as well as from other parts of Africa. The newcomers brought their indigenous foods and tastes, some of which have entered into the mainstream of Provençal and French food.

When we first came to Provence, we were surprised to find a colony of Algerians in the next village, housed in two long rows of single-story cream-colored stuccoed buildings, each small apartment with identical brown doors and shutters. The women had hennaed hands and wore long skirts in several layers. The men, whom we often saw more often, wore blue workers' pants or jeans. When we asked about them, we were told that they were Harkis, Algerians who had supported the French in the Algerian war for independence and had chosen to come to France rather than stay in Algeria. The French government had provided housing for the Harkis, work for the men, and the benefits of the French social system for their families, including public education.

We met some of the men in the vineyards during the grape harvest the first fall we were in Provence. Their food made a huge impression on Ethel, who was with us in the vineyards, and she recalls with clarity the fragrance, taste, and appearance of the blood orange one of the men segmented and gave to her. She also remembers the *merguez* sausage she was given off the grill when the men cooked their lunch.

Merguez, the spicy North African lamb sausage, is to the Provençal barbecue grill what hot dogs are to the American. The finger-slim, dark orange sausages are sold in bulk in supermarkets and are artisanally made in butcher shops. They are found throughout France, just like another North African dish, couscous. Couscous, which often includes chunks of lamb or grilled *merguez*, is part of the scent of the open markets of Provence, where vendors cook it in vast, round-bottomed pots. The smell of the vegetables simmering in spicy, harissa-laced broth makes me want to stop and buy it immediately, and I often give in to the impulse. The couscous is sold in portion sizes from one to eight, neatly packaged in plastic take-away boxes, just like paella, another import to the marketplace, this one from Spain.

In France, I can buy all the *merguez* I want, but in California it's hard to come by, so I've learned to make it myself. I put chunks of lamb shoulder, garlic, paprika, salt, pepper, cayenne, and thyme in my food processor and pulse to get a medium-coarse texture, or run the mixture through my sausage grinder. Next I bring out my stand mixer, fit it with the sausage attachment, and stuff lengths of small sausage casings, tying them off one by one. I cook some fresh on the grill the same day I make them, and freeze the rest. Each bite of my homemade *merguez* is a taste of my Provençal life.

....

Of all the lamb dishes I have eaten or prepared in Provence, *méchoui* stands out, not only for the food, but for the camaraderie surrounding it. It began with Ibn.

Ibn was the all-purpose servant of M. Meille, a former military man with what he called "enterprises" in the Côte d'Ivoire. M. Meille had purchased the house on the hillside above the place that Joanne, Donald, and I once owned together. He was rarely seen, but Ibn was out every day, clearing brush, digging trenches, taking care of the dogs, moving rocks, chopping wood. Joanne and her husband, Guild, came to know him initially, as we did, through the children.

Ibn, swathed in brightly colored robes as he worked on the hillside with a scythe or an ax, was an exotic in the Provençal landscape, and Ethel, Oliver, and Alexandra, Joanne and Guild's daughter, were fascinated by him. He told them stories, illustrating them in grand gestures with his pink-palmed hands. From the deep folds of his robes he pulled out wrapped candies for the children, who were always puzzled about where he kept them, since they could see no pockets. They learned that he had a family of his own back in Africa.

As we talked with Ibn over the summer, we noticed he spoke a lot about the food back home and the kinds of things he cooked. That was when we learned about the *méchoui*.

"It is a big feast we make. We take a nice lamb, not too big, not too small, fill it with much rice and vegetables, and roast it slowly, slowly on a spit over a fire. You would like it, I think. It is very, very good and there are many sheep here, like in my country."

We were fascinated by the concept, and as we questioned him about how to do it, we decided to plan a feast under Ibn's guidance, which we would have at Joanne and Guild's house.

Donald and I knew a sheep rancher near Esparron where we thought we could buy a lamb of the ideal size. Ibn said he could construct a spit, and Joanne and Guild helped him choose a site not too far from the house to dig a fire pit. "We need good wood," Ibn told us. "Hard wood, like oak. Nice and dry too. Not fresh."

We chose a date, a Sunday two weeks away, and proceeded to make the invitation list, coming up with about thirty people, including our neighbors Marie and Marcel, and Adèle and Pascal, and our old friends, the Brunos.

The day before the *méchoui*, Donald and I drove to a farm where a freshly killed and dressed lamb was waiting for us. Donald and a worker at the farm carried the carcass, one holding the rear legs, the other the front. We had prepared for the trip by folding the rear seats of the car forward to make more room and covering the back with a tarp in which to wrap the lamb.

We drove directly to Joanne and Guild's and stored the wrapped lamb in their *cave* until the next morning when it would be stuffed and put on the spit. Joanne had assembled all the ingredients for the stuffing, and that evening, with Ibn's help, we cooked nearly three kilos of rice, chopped the vegetables and sautéed them in olive oil, then mixed everything together with the minced heart, kidneys, and liver. We added various seasonings—cayenne, pepper, salt, harissa, turmeric, and cumin—tasted the stuffing, adding more seasonings, and tasted again, until Ibn declared, "Yes. Now it is right. Now it tastes like my country."

Every pot and basin in the house was full of stuffing. We covered them and put them in the *cave* along with the lamb, which we had slathered with olive oil, harissa, and wild thyme, according to Ibn's instruction. All was ready to go for the next day.

Donald left in the early-morning light to go start the fire with Ibn, coming back for me and the children later. By the time we arrived, the lamb, already becoming golden, was turning on the spit above a deep pit of coals. Ibn was standing next to the spit, basting the lamb with a brush he had constructed by fastening branches of wild rosemary and thyme to a thin length of oak branch with heavy twine. Next to him was a bowl of the harissa-laden marinade we had made the night before. I could smell the herbs and spices, and hear the fat hissing as it dripped onto the coals. It was already a memorable day.

The roasting lamb kept us company as we fronted the entire width of the house with a line of tables. Since one end of the line was exposed to the sun, Guild had devised a canopy of sorts by hanging a Indian bedspread between a mulberry tree and two poles anchored in the ground. We set the table with an assortment of Provençal printed tablecloths and a combination of my dishes and Joanne's. We had *rosé* and red wine from the local cooperative and loads of bread. Joanne and I had made old-fashioned deep-dish peach pies for dessert. By the time people started arriving at noon, the lamb was nearly done, and we started pouring *pastis* and eating olives.

When it was ready, the cooked lamb, spit and all, was moved to a table set up near the fire pit. Ibn cut the wire holding the lamb to the spit, then clipped and pulled out the wire that held the belly together, releasing the aroma of the spiced stuffing, which mingled with the crispy scent of the roasted meat. With a long-handled spoon, he scooped the stuffing away from the spit and into bowls. With everyone gathered around to watch the process, Ibn removed the spit, which he had made from two pieces of pipe. He finished scooping the stuffing, reaching deep into the cavity to ensure that every bit made it to the table. We covered the bowls and put them near the embers of the fire to keep them warm while Ibn carved the meat and heaped slices of leg and shoulder, chops, and ribs on platters.

The guests helped carry the serving dishes to the table, and before the plates were passed around, a standing toast was drunk to Ibn for cooking this feast with us.

I savored every bite. The crunchy skin, which had become mahogany with the long basting, was my favorite. The harissa made it spicy, but I could taste and smell the rosemary and thyme, too. The rosy pink meat was just right and dripped juice that during the cooking had moistened the stuffing, and the vegetables in the stuffing had virtually melted into the rice during the long cooking. We all ate until the platters and bowls were nearly empty, scraping our plates clean with our bread, and finished the last of the wine.

Joanne and I had prepared greens for salads, but people were too full, so instead of serving salad, we cleared the dishes and waited awhile before bringing out pie and coffee, allowing everyone to take a stroll or a nap, typical in Provence following a long meal.

After dessert, the adults stayed at the table, sipping coffee as the sun began to drop behind the house, unwilling for the evening to end.

I have fond memories of that singular Sunday when friends came together to cook a *méchoui*, now a common feast in the area. The next year Ibn didn't return with M. Meille, who would only say that Ibn had gone away. The fire pit, used once or twice again for barbecuing chops, was eventually filled in. Today, a dry space with sparse grass marks where it once was, just enough for Joanne and me to see in our mind's eye the lamb turning on its spit, our children playing, our friends gathered, and Ibn smiling as he watched it all.

Gigot d'agneau aux herbes de Provence

LEG OF LAMB WITH ROSEMARY, THYME, AND LAVENDER

As the butcher's wife says, it's always a pleasure to have a nice leg of lamb, and I agree. Rosy, juicy meat, well flavored with garlic, thyme, rosemary, and winter savory, is as fine a dish as you can hope for. Slow-cooked white beans and seasoned, broiled tomato halves complete the dish for me.

Preheat the oven to 400 degrees F. Choose a leg of lamb that weighs 4½ to 5 pounds. Rub it all over with olive oil and plenty of coarse sea salt and freshly ground black pepper. Next, gently pat on enough *herbes de Provence* to cover it. The lamb should be well seasoned. This is no time to be shy. If you don't have *herbes de Provence*, make a mixture of two-thirds dried thyme, one-third dried rosemary or winter savory, and one-third dried lavender. Using a knife, make a deep slit in the lamb and insert a thin sliver of fresh garlic. Repeat until you've inserted about twenty slivers of garlic.

Place the lamb on a rack in a roasting pan. Roast, basting several times with the cooking juices, until the lamb is golden brown and has begun to pull away from the bone, and the meat bounces back when pushed with a finger, 50 to 60 minutes. It doesn't take very long to cook, especially if you like your lamb rare to medium-rare, as I do. To make certain I'm not over- or undercooking it, I insert an instant-read thermometer into the thickest part of the leg, but not touching the bone. It should register 125 degrees F to 130 degrees F for medium-rare. If medium is desired, roast for another 15 minutes, or until the thermometer registers 135 degrees F to 145 degrees F. Remove to a cutting board, cover loosely with foil, and let stand for 15 to 20 minutes.

While the lamb is resting, remove any fat from the pan juices. Heat the juices, still in the roasting pan, over medium-high heat, add a little red wine, and reduce the juices. Carve the lamb into thin slices and put them on a warmed platter. Reserve the juices from the carving and pour them into the roasting pan, bring to a boil, and pour over the sliced lamb.

SERVES 8 TO 10

CHAPTER 8

WEDDING TARTS

Cooking for a village. The Mayor dresses up. Lost dancer.

I arrived in Nice at 2:10 in the afternoon, on the Air France flight from San Francisco that I habitually take, but without the habitual load of books, new cookware, and the dual-season clothes that I usually migrate with now. This time I had only one bag lightly packed with a swimsuit, a couple pairs of linen pants, a few tops, a sweater, and two dresses suitable for a French summer wedding. The wedding gift, a pale green glass cake pedestal, was in my carry-on. Later I would realize that I should have brought a hat, a fancy, ribbon-bedecked, broad-brimmed hat.

When I drove up the familiar winding road to my house, I could see a dozen or more cars parked helter-skelter across the road at the Lamys'. It was going to be a big family wedding, with all the extended members in attendance. Robert and Françoise Lamy, almost eighty, were beginning to slow down a bit and I suspected this might be the last big, intact family event. Instead of putting on the wedding feast at the family home, as for previous weddings, this one would be at the *salle des fêtes* for only close friends and family, with the ritual postceremony *apéritif* for most of the village held at home.

I opened up the house, turning the heavy key in the lock of the front door, and went directly into the kitchen. A bowl of peaches was on the table with a note from Françoise under it, inviting me to dinner at seven. I ate one of the juicy peaches, made myself a cup of coffee, then went upstairs and unpacked.

At seven, someone, probably one of the grandchildren, rang the big brass gong the Lamys use to call large groups of family to meals. A minute later, when I walked across the road, more than two dozen people were collected around and under the four spreading mulberry trees that shaded the vast flagstone terrace. Robert and his sons were pouring *apéritifs*, offering *pastis, vin d'orange*, or *kir*, while several of the younger granddaughters were passing bowls of nuts and olives, in between eating them. Long tables covered in an assortment of cloths were set in an L shape.

Just as I arrived, Françoise came out of the kitchen with a platter stacked double with *tapenade* toasts. With her short cropped gray hair, round blue eyes, and soft olive skin, and wearing her classic polo shirt, she looked the same to me as the first time I had met her more than thirty years ago when Donald and I lived down the road with our children and she bought the goat cheese we made. She put down her tray and, after we exchanged kisses, took my hands in hers and asked about me and my family.

Her grandson Laurent, the groom-to-be, looked not much different than when he had spent part of a summer with me and Jim in California at age fifteen. Only now, at twenty-three, he was taller. His thick dark hair still shot out at incorrigible angles, and his black-rimmed glasses were perched at that same slight tilt on his nose. His face, square jawed like his grandfather's, broke into a shy smile when he saw me.

"Georgeanne! I can't believe you came all the way from California, just for the wedding. My parents say you're staying only six days." He introduced his bride-to-be to me, a plump blonde with blue eyes and freckles, as talkative as he was introverted.

When it was time to be seated, Robert said I should sit next to him. "That's yours." He patted the pink-and-yellow floral print napkin holder set at my place. "You'll be here all week, like the rest of the family."

Thereafter, I could always tell my place, which changed with each meal, by my napkin holder, a tangible symbol to me that I belonged to this large, complex, and kindly family.

The younger grandchildren brought the first course to the tables, big bowls of sliced tomatoes from the garden, mixed with tuna, chopped eggs, and red onion and dressed with lots of olive oil, salt, and pepper. Robert doesn't like vinegar, so it was absent. We all had at least two helpings, sopping up the juices on our plate with the abundant bread, cleaning our plates for the main dish, which was rice with *ratatouille* made with eggplants, peppers, zucchini, tomatoes, and basil from the garden just on the other side of the terrace where we were eating.

We sat until late under the mulberries, as we always do, sipping our wine and finishing our cheese and fruit. The younger children had cleared the table and started the dishwasher and were now off in their own world.

The moon, nearly full, illuminated the wheat fields and vineyards around us as we sat talking about the next day. More extended family on both sides were arriving, some in the morning, others later.

"So, we'll need to prepare lunch and dinner tomorrow— we'll be around thirty. We also need to fill and cook the tarts, and make the *tapenade* and *anchoïade* for the wedding *apéritif* party. We'll be about one hundred twenty people for the *apéritif,* and we've already made the eight hundred tart shells we need," said Delphine, the eldest granddaughter, twenty-eight, who was in charge of the *apéritif* foods. Like her brother she had spent part of a summer with me and Jim, and she and I had shared many food adventures in both California and France, including cooking live lobsters, digging potatoes, and planting vegetable gardens.

"It's our last day to prepare, because the day after we have to be at the *mairie* at eleven," she announced.

Marriage, by law a civil ceremony in France and the only legally valid one, takes place at the *mairie,* the city hall, which sometimes has a specifically designated *salle de mariage.* A religious ceremony is an option, but has no legal status in the eyes of the state. The civil ceremony is not unlike being in court, but the attendees are better dressed and generally include only the most immediate family, or intimate friends, depending on the size of the city hall and whether or not there will be a church ceremony as well. Donald and I had been married at the *salle de mariage* at the *mairie* in Aix-en-Provence, but that was a much larger setting than a village city hall.

The next morning, after a jet-lagged sleep behind my shuttered windows in the deep silence of the countryside, I went across the road to help. It was 9:30 and the tables under the mulberries held the remains of morning *café au lait,* bread, butter, jam, and cereal bowls. These were quickly cleared, and cutting boards and knives set out. Dinner that night was to be a big couscous.

"We'll finish all the cooking this morning, then this afternoon we're going down to the community center to decorate," Delphine told me after the morning round of kisses. Then it was time to get to work on the couscous.

"Georgeanne, toi, tu coupe les carottes. Tatie, tu coupe les cour-gettes." She gave us each a task—chopping the onions, garlic, carrots, zucchini, and green beans—while she prepared the restaurant-size pot of chicken and the broth, adding local garbanzo beans that Françoise had purchased the previous fall. As we finished chopping the vegetables, she added those.

209

Françoise's kitchen easily held the six of us around the long wooden table that served for both working and eating. The kitchen had been modernized several times, but the glossy, dark red tiles on the long counter holding the sink, dishwasher, and cooktop remained. The wall behind the counter, red tiles as well, is fitted with two built-in ovens. Above them is a shelf where she keeps a collection of old Provençal terra-cotta cookware. Best of all, the kitchen has a generous, thigh-low window that opens on the terrace. Light pours into the kitchen, and Françoise sets her flats of vegetables and fruits from the garden on the sill, working out of them as she cooks.

That morning the kitchen quickly gave up its smell of morning coffee to that of chicken and herbs and by eleven the broth for the couscous, rich with vegetables and tender chicken, was gently bubbling on the stove. All that remained was to cook the couscous itself that evening, just before serving, and for the men to grill the *merguez* sausages that would be part of the dish.

Delphine and her designated crew of cousins, clad in shorts and bathing suits, had been diligently at work in the dining room, forming an assembly line circling the large round pearwood table, which was covered in plastic to protect it. They were filling bite-size tarts with various fillings, then storing the cooked tarts in boxes as they laughed and chatted. Delphine had made a classic *quiche* filling with a savory custard and Gruyère cheese and another with creamed spinach, and the crew spooned the fillings directly into the partially baked shells. Some of the shells were being spread first with mustard before being filled and topped with slices of cherry tomatoes.

"Oh, that one was my mother's idea. The mustard flavors the custard without being mixed into it. We're making big tarts for lunch today, with the same filling as the little tarts, so you can taste everything then. Here, can you start filling the lunch tarts?" She indicated a stack of eight tart tins, each with a lightly golden, partially baked shell.

"Make three of the tomato—I know everyone likes those, and I bet you will too."

I followed Delphine's instructions, brushing a thin layer of pungent Amora mustard on the bottom of three tarts, ladling in the filling, and then covering the surface with fat slices of tomato.

"Drizzle a little olive oil on, then some fresh thyme—it's over there." She pointed to a bowl of fresh thyme leaves, all the stems removed.

"Nice," I said as I picked up the bowl, inhaling the resinous aroma. "Who cleaned the thyme?"

"The little boys." She nodded toward two of her cousins, about seven or eight years old. "We sent them out to cut it. They watched cartoons while they cleaned it. I told them no TV unless they cleaned the thyme."

We cooked the lunch tarts in pairs and when we had finished our *apéritif*, this time rum, over ice, from l'Île de la Réunion, where Robert had been the *préfet*, or governor, during the 1970s, all the tarts had been baked, and the expected guests had arrived. Françoise rang the gong. I found my napkin holder between one of the younger cousins and Robert's sister, an old friend of mine. We agreed that the tomato tart had an added piquancy, but it was so subtle that we would never have guessed that it came from mustard. A huge green salad was served with the tarts, and we had our choice of red, *rosé*, or white wine from the bottles set at intervals on the tables. Sliced melons were brought to the table for dessert. Afterward, some of us, me included, opted for coffee, while others took a nap in the lounge chairs in the shade near the swimming pool.

That afternoon I went with assorted aunts, cousins, and in-laws-to-be to decorate the *salle des fêtes*. It sits on the village square with the *mairie*, across from the defunct wine cooperative, and next door to the one-room school where I once drank Champagne and ate cake with the other parents at the school Christmas party when Oliver was just a baby and Denys Fine the teacher.

The *salle des fêtes*, which has the same functional, uninspired architecture as the school and the co-op, consists of a large, empty room and a big commercial kitchen. We set about transforming the space for the wedding feast and dance.

The girls climbed ladders and hung garlands of twisted green, gold, and white crepe from the overhead lights. I helped set up the folding tables and chairs and covered the tables with green, gold, and white cloths. The girls, once finished with the garlands, put small glass jars they had filled with bouquets of lavender and wheat on all the tables, two or three per table.

Some of the women were busily making up packets of white-sugar-coated almonds, the *dragées*, in green net and tying them with yellow satin ribbon. Sugar-coated almonds are traditional for weddings, baptisms, and communions and are handed out or placed at every table setting, a memento to take home. In candy store windows, you'll often see ready-made net packets filled with *dragées* in pastel shades of pink, blue, green, and yellow, as well as white.

At six, when we left, the *salle des fêtes* was fully decorated, and the tables set. A space had been cleared for dancing, and the refrigerators filled with the olives, bite-size *pâtés* in puff pastry, smoked salmon, beef tenderloins, roasted red peppers, marinated eggplants and artichokes, salad greens, and cheeses that would be served buffet style the night of the party. The wine and Champagne had already been delivered and were chilling in the cold room next to the kitchen.

That night, over couscous, I learned that I was included in the family group that would accompany the bride and groom to city hall the next morning where they would be married by the mayor. I was to be ready at 10:30.

Of my two dresses, I decided on the pale green crepe with short sleeves, with a pair of strappy, copper-colored sandals. More suitable for daytime wear, I told myself. I'd save the short black one to wear to the evening party. Laurent's three sisters and his mother, father, and grandparents were all ready when I arrived.

Laurent's sisters—he was the only boy of five siblings—were wearing long satin dresses in shades of mauve, rose, and blue, and matching wide-brimmed hats of organza and silk. Françoise and Laurent's mother wore simple dresses, but no hats. Ah, I thought, not everyone will be wearing hats, already regretting the vintage black wide-brimmed hat with pink satin roses I had left behind in California. When Laurent's aunts joined us, they all wore what I've come to call French wedding hats—hats of the most extravagant confection that I normally see only in movies or in the celebrity photographs in French magazines.

"*Ah, mes belles filles,*" said Robert, the patriarch, proudly. "What a lovely array of hats. All women should wear beautiful hats at weddings."

The women in the bride's entourage also wore glamorous hats. The bride's, a wide-brimmed silk in creamy white that allowed wisps of her piled-up hair to escape, matched her white brocade suit.

We climbed into various cars and made the three-minute drive down the road to city hall where we were escorted into the mayor's office by his secretary. The office was just large enough for six chairs, the mayor's desk, and the French flag, and allowed standing room for everyone else.

Laurent, his bride, and their flanking parents took the six chairs in front of the desk, and the rest of us lined up behind them. Minutes later the mayor appeared, looking more regal and official than I had ever seen him, dressed in a dark suit with a tie. Across his chest was the wide red, white, and blue satin ribbon, complete with rosette, of the French République.

He greeted us with kisses or handshakes, depending on whether he knew us, then opened the small ceremony with a few words acknowledging his modesty at performing an official *cérémonie de l'état* before a dignitary such as his friend Robert Lamy, the former *préfet* of Champagne and la Réunion. We all laughed a little and then the mayor began asking the official questions of the couple and their parents demanded by the state. Papers were filled out, signed, and passed back and forth, and the couple was pronounced man and wife.

Later that day, as I stood on the steps of the sixteenth-century church in the *vieux village* with the rest of the guests, waiting for the bride and groom to emerge into the late-afternoon light, my thoughts went back to the other Lamy wedding I had attended with Donald, Ethel, and Oliver. We hadn't known we were invited until we arrived for our annual summer sojourn and were given an invitation for the wedding, only a week away.

That time, more than twenty-five years ago, a hundred or more of us were waiting on the same church steps and in its courtyard, dressed in our summer finery. Baskets of ribbon-tied packets of rice had been passed around by little girls in smooth pink dresses. When the double doors of the church were flung back and the groom came through, arm in arm with his new bride, we undid the ribbons and showered them with rice as they hurried down the steps to the back of a truck decorated with garlands of ivy, geraniums, white lace flowers, and long streams of white and lavender ribbons.

The groom lifted his bride by her waist and set her onto the tailgate of the truck. She was a vision from a fairy tale with her dark olive skin, black hair, and green eyes catching the light of the late-afternoon sun, and her dress, a bouffant of white tulle, surrounding her like clouds. Her veil, attached to a crown of white flowers, billowed behind her, and her ankles were crossed, showing little white sandals. Handsome in full morning-coat attire, complete with top hat and a *boutonnière* of lavender, her new husband was the perfect escort.

Once settled in their modern-day version of a Provençal wedding cart, they started off on the single-lane road that snakes from the perched village to the Lamy home. We and all the other guests followed the couple, who were merrily blowing kisses and waving from the back of the truck, honking and joining in the cacophony that escorted them.

We parked our car down the road from our house, letting other guests have the closer parking spot we normally used. Walking toward our house we could already hear the music coming from the Lamys'. The sun had begun to dip behind the *roc de bidau*, the rock outcropping that overlooks our little valley, bringing the lavender glow that pervades the countryside during the long summer dusk. White lights, strung across the patio and through the mulberry trees, around the new swimming pool, and back again along the top of the cypress hedge, were already lit.

Set back on the deep lawn were long tables covered in white linen and decorated with small bouquets of lavender and greenery. Robert's mother was still alive then, a small woman dressed in black as always, and she sat in the center with several other women of her generation, while the younger children were running and playing. Robert, tall and handsome in his summer linen suit, jacket now removed, was serving planter's punch. I remembered it from my parents' days and had only two glasses.

"Ah, c'est très bien," he said when I declined a third glass. "We have wonderful wine tonight, cases of Grand Cru Bourgogne, a wedding gift from the bride's uncle who owns a *domaine* in Burgundy. It's *superbe*." He laughed. "I know because we opened several bottles last night."

Platters of samosas, the folded and fried pastry packets that Françoise had learned to make while living in Réunion, and that had become a Lamy family tradition, were passed around. Rolled-up slices of ham filled with cheese and capers, and toasts topped with spreads of sweet peppers and eggplant, smoked salmon, or smoked herring completed the appetizers.

To be honest, I don't remember the meal, which became a blur after the appetizers and the wine. A magnificent tiered wedding cake was eventually cut and we toasted the bride and groom with Champagne. Under twinkling lights and the stars we danced until two in the morning. Donald danced with Robert's mother and Françoise, as well as with Ethel and Aileen, Georgette Fine, and Marie Palazolli, and with me, of course. Ethel and I danced with the Lamy sons, with Robert, Denys

Fine and his sons, and several of the bride's male relatives we didn't know. Oliver would allow only the bride, on whom he had a crush, to dance with him.

....

Now I was back at a Lamy wedding, this time helping behind the scenes as well as being a guest. All my family had been invited, but I was the only one able to come.

As I waited there on the steps, I half expected to see a flower-bedecked truck pull up in front of the church, but instead it was a white *deux chevaux,* driven by Delphine's boyfriend and decorated with streamers of green and gold ribbon. The newly married couple hurried down the steps, laughing as they dodged the rice we threw at them, and climbed into the waiting car, the streamers waving behind it as it pulled away from the church and followed the winding road to the family home.

About one hundred fifty people, including nearly half the village's entire population, gathered at the Lamys' for the cele-bratory *apéritif.* I spent the early part of the party in the kitchen, keeping the *hors d'oeuvre* trays amply filled with the tarts we had made and spreading *tapenade* on toasts. When most of the tarts and toasts had been served and I emerged to join the party, I realized that I knew most of the people, many for more than half my life.

Some had been children when I first met them, hiding behind their mother's skirts like Ethel and Oliver. Others were farmers and their wives, plumbers, electricians, and masons with whom I've had a nodding or better acquaintance since first coming to the village. Some, like Adèle and Pascal and Marie and Marcel, were among my best friends. Others were relative newcomers that I had come to know later. There were people

I had dinner with long ago, whose faces, but not their names, I remembered. Others were community fixtures, the remaining members of a generation almost gone. A good part were the sons, daughters, grandsons and granddaughters, cousins, brothers, sisters, and attendant spouses of Robert and Françoise, most of whom I knew well.

After an hour or so, the guests began to drift away, except for those of us invited to the *fête de mariage* at the community center. I drove down on my own, suspecting I might want to leave earlier than some of my compatriots. I arrived about the same time as everyone else, about sixty-five of us, and Marie grabbed my arm, saying, "Let's sit together."

I shared a table with Marie and Marcel and an assortment of Lamy relatives, including Robert's brother and sister, feeling more than ever a part of the family.

Platters of smoked salmon, *pâté* in puff pastry, *cornichons*, thin slices of salt-cured ham, almonds, and olives had been set on all the tables, and we served ourselves the first course, passing the platters among us, commenting on the wedding, how happy Laurent looked, and how good the wine was.

When the first course was finished, Marie and I got up and went back to the kitchen to help the caterers, friends of ours from the village. We arranged thin slices of cold beef tenderloin on one set of trays, thin slices of cold sliced pork on another, garnishing all with quartered tomatoes and sprigs of basil from Françoise's garden. Then we brought the trays out to buffet tables already groaning with bowls of roasted red peppers and eggplants, tomato and mozzarella salad, potato salad, and green salad, all liberally dressed in olive oil.

Recorded music had been playing when we arrived at the hall, then stopped for the first course, starting up again about the same time Marie and I had headed into the kitchen. It was music that could be called suitable for all ages: waltzes intermingled with American rock 'n' roll classics from the 1960s and 1970s, French cabaret songs, and world music. By the time the platters of local goat cheese, Camembert, Brie, Époisses, and Roquefort had been fully sampled, the music began again, and Laurent and his bride opened the dance floor, followed by family members, young and old. An hour or more later, after a three-tiered chocolate-raspberry wedding cake from the local bakery had been cut and served, world music dominated, and all the young people were dancing, dresses flying, high-heeled sandals kicked off under the tables and jackets hanging from chairs.

Marie and I both wanted to dance, but Marcel and the other men at our table would have none of it. Finally, the two of us simply joined the people on the dance floor, as did other women accompanied by reluctant men and the young children.

While we were dancing Françoise and Robert slipped away. Marcel came onto the dance floor and told Marie he wanted to go home, so I left too.

As I lay in bed, snug in a bedroom familiar to me for half my life, looking at the ceiling of hand-hewn planks and the smooth, plastered walls lined with bookshelves, I thought how lucky I was to have such a life, one in California, another here. In just six weeks I'd be back, bags loaded, to teach another series of cooking classes. But first I'd spend time picking tomatoes and melons and cooking with Marie and Françoise and enjoying long, leisurely meals with all my friends who have become my extended family.

Tarte aux tomates

TOMATO TART

This is the tart I helped make for the Lamy wedding. As promised, the mustard base doesn't have a strong taste, but offers a little something extra that makes the tart exceptional. We used purchased, ready-to-roll fresh pie dough available in many different versions all over France. I love this concept, and everyone I know uses the dough for both sweet and savory tarts. I've found a similar fresh product in my local supermarket in California, as well as some very good, ready-to-roll frozen products. If ready-made dough isn't available or you don't want to use it, choose a favorite pie dough recipe to make these tarts.

Preheat an oven to 400 degrees F. Roll out the dough to about 14 inches in diameter and less than ¼ inch thick. Put the dough in a tart pan 1 inch deep and 12 inches in diameter with a removable bottom. Pat the dough firmly into the bottom and up the sides of the pan, then trim the edges even with the rim.

Spread the bottom with a thin layer of Dijon mustard, then cover with a single layer of snugly packed tomato slices. Drizzle with extra-virgin olive oil and sprinkle with a little fine sea salt, freshly ground black pepper, and fresh thyme. Top with grated Gruyère. Bake until the crust is golden and the tomatoes have collapsed, 20 to 25 minutes. Remove the tart to a rack and let it cool for 20 minutes or so before slicing it into wedges.

SERVES 6

In the twilight of the vaulted room, the fireplace looms, prom-
ising warmth and companionship on this October evening.
I've built a fire of oak and pine deep in the hearth, and when the
wood is burnt down to glowing chunks, I'll put on a handful or
two of grape prunings and grill my lamb chops. They're sitting on
a plate in the kitchen, rubbed with olive oil and sprinkled with
wild thyme. I've already been to the garden to pick young *frisée*,
arugula, and thick stalks of white-ribbed chard. The greens are
washed now, sitting in the enameled colander, a wedding present
I brought here long ago from California. A fresh goat cheese, like
the ones I used to make, is resting in the refrigerator. Soon I'll
broil it to put on top of my salad.

I pour myself a glass of *rosé* and sip it while I cook the chard
and make a *béchamel* sauce. I put out a few olives, black and
green, in a little bowl I bought at the market with Jim the previous year. It's pale yellow and I like the way the olives look in it.

The chard, mixed with the *béchamel* and topped with bread
crumbs and butter, is baking, so I set the wooden table in front
of the fireplace with my favorite antique French napkins, huge,
heavily embroidered squares that once were part of someone's
trousseau. One, folded in half, serves as a place mat, the other as
it was intended. I open the glass-fronted armoire and bring out
two brown-rimmed, mustard-gold plates, part of the set Marie
gave me as a housewarming gift when electricity and plumbing

were finally installed. An antique silver knife and fork from a flea market finish the table setting, along with a water glass, a pitcher, and a terra-cotta dish to hold the wine bottle. I'll bring the small bowls of sea salt and pepper later, bowls like the one the olives are in. A small glass vase set in the middle of the table holds the red and golden grape leaves I picked earlier from the vineyard that borders the garden.

The aroma of the *gratin* tells me it's almost ready. The timing is perfect. The coals are glowing, ready to cook the lamb. My grill consists of a long-legged wrought-iron trivet I inherited with the house, on which I put a grilling rack, set over the hottest part of the coals. The lamb sizzles when I set it on the grill and I can already taste the promise of crisp bits of fat and the rosy meat infused with the fragrance of the thyme. I pour a little more wine while I tend the chops, turning them several times. Just before the chops are ready, I broil the cheese.

As soon as the chops are done, I move them to a plate set on the hearth. They'll rest and stay warm while I have my salad, dressed with olive oil from Robert Lamy's brother and my home-made vinegar, topped with the broiled goat cheese.

Sitting down to my salad, I look through the window and see the sky has turned deep violet, announcing the dark and the silence to come. I've never been anywhere as quiet as my house in Provence, set deep in the countryside amid small patches of vineyards and wheat carved out of the surrounding forests of oak, pine, and juniper.

The cheese is hot, slightly runny at the edges where it blends with the vinaigrette and catches the leaves of *frisée* and arugula. I finish the last bit on my plate, cleaning it with a piece of *baguette* and a deep sigh of contentment.

I'd forgotten a hot pad, so I put that on the table first, then set down my chard *gratin*, baked in the small, dark red rectangular baking dish that my mother-in-law bought for me when she and her husband came to visit, flying from San Francisco to Nice. It was the last trip they made together, and the only thing she acquired on the journey.

Before bringing the lamb chops to the table, I put another piece of wood on the fire. It is too cheerful to let it die out. The chops are perfectly cooked, and their juices mingle on the plate with the creamy *gratin*. I cut the meat close to the bone and, at the end, pick the bone up to chew the edges, savoring the last of the fat and meat.

I don't usually eat dessert, but tonight I'm having the remnant half of an almond-walnut caramel pastry I bought at a *pâtisserie* in Aups. I ate the other half around four, with a cup of coffee. Tonight I'll have a little red wine with it while I read the first pages of Trollope's *Barchester Towers*. It's been a long time since I first read it, nearly thirty years, and taking it down from my bookshelf in the bedroom upstairs and turning the pages once again was like meeting an old friend. I'll read it at breakfast too, while I drink dark, rich coffee with hot milk, and eat a slice of fresh bread with butter and homemade cherry jam. If it's chilly, I'll build another fire. Maybe I'll read all morning while a beef *daube* simmers on the back of the stove. With only a few days left before returning home to my husband and California, I want to make the most of my time alone in my house in Provence.